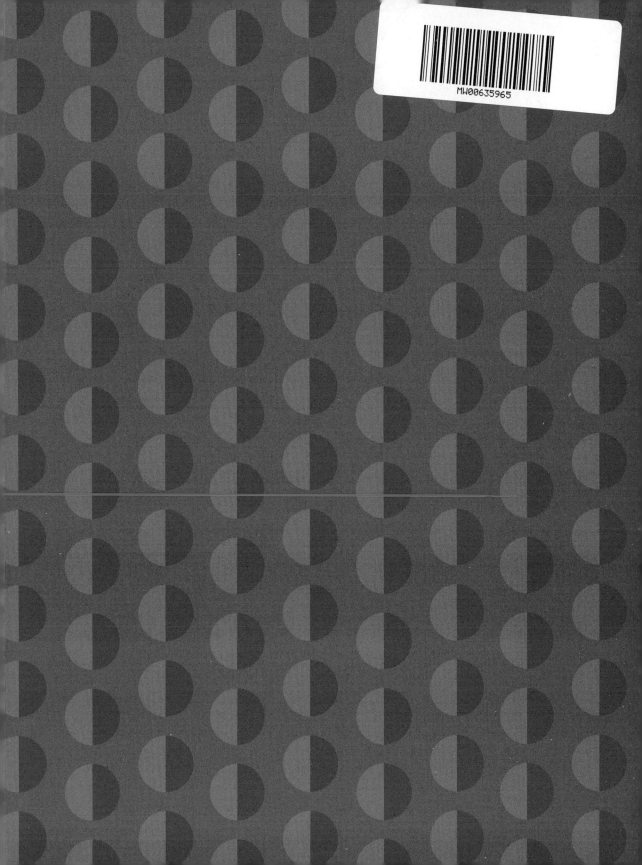

30-SECOND
LITERATURE

30-SECOND LITERATURE

The 50 most important forms, genres and styles, each explained in half a minute

Editor
Ella Berthoud

Contributors
Naomi Frisby
Lauren de Sá Naylor
Valerie O'Riordan
Charlotte Raby
Lucien Young

Illustrator
Nicky Ackland-Snow

IVY PRESS

First published in the UK in 2020 by
Ivy Press
An imprint of The Quarto Group
The Old Brewery, 6 Blundell Street
London N7 9BH, United Kingdom
T (0)20 7700 6700
www.QuartoKnows.com

British Library Cataloguing-in-
Publication Data
A catalogue record for this
book is available from the
British Library.

ISBN: 978-1-78240-844-4

This book was conceived,
designed and produced by
Ivy Press
58 West Street, Brighton BN1 2RA, UK

Publisher **David Breuer**
Editorial Director **Tom Kitch**
Art Director **James Lawrence**
Commissioning Editor **Kate Shanahan**
Design Manager **Anna Stevens**
Designer **Ginny Zeal**
Picture Researcher **Sharon Dortenzio**
Illustrator **Nicky Ackland-Snow**

Cover images: Shutterstock/ Ewa Studio;
alexblacksea; Andrej Antic

Printed in China

10 9 8 7 6 5 4 3 2 1

CONTENTS

6 Introduction

10 History of Literature
12 GLOSSARY
14 The oral tradition
16 Early literature
18 Sanskrit literature
20 Medieval literature
22 Early modern literature
24 Modern literature
26 **Profile: Hilda Doolittle**
28 Modernist literature
30 Postcolonial literature

32 The Novel
34 GLOSSARY
36 The birth of the novel
38 Epistolary novel
40 Historical novel
42 Science fiction
44 Crime
46 **Profile: Fyodor Dostoevsky**
48 Horror
50 Utopia/Dystopia
52 Fantasy
54 Romance
56 Graphic novel
58 Young adult
60 LGBTQ+

62 Literary Prose
64 GLOSSARY
66 Short story
68 Diary
70 Autobiography & memoir
72 **Profile: Chimamanda Ngozi Adichie**
74 Philosophical works
76 Religious texts

78 Poetry
80 GLOSSARY
82 Epic poem
84 Free verse
86 Sonnet
88 Ode
90 **Profile: Hafez**
92 Ballad
94 Haiku
96 Ghazal

98 Drama
100 GLOSSARY
102 Tragedy
104 Comedy
106 **Profile: Aristophanes**
108 Melodrama
110 Theatre of the absurd
112 Passion play
114 Political play

116 Literary Devices
118 GLOSSARY
120 Irony
122 Allegory
124 **Profile: Jorge Luis Borges**
126 Symbolism
128 Anthropomorphism
130 Personification
132 Foreshadow & flashback

134 Literary Styles
136 GLOSSARY
138 Narrative voice
140 Realism
142 **Profile: Ali Smith**
144 Satire
146 Gothic
148 Postmodernism
150 Stream of consciousness

152 Appendices
154 Resources
156 Notes on contributors
158 Index
160 Acknowledgements

INTRODUCTION
Ella Berthoud

Literature is imagination in the form of words on paper, or simply memorized and recited. It crosses borders, both physical and mental, allowing us to travel beyond our limitations. A time machine that gives us instant access to the minds of writers from thousands of years ago, it offers multiple alternative presents and numerous possible futures. Through literature, as readers we gain insight into worlds we could never have dreamt of, giving us the opportunity to understand other cultures, other ways of thinking or being or living. We read to find ourselves, and we read to understand others, to gain empathy and to enrich our minds and souls.

Since the birth of the novel we have been able to discover ourselves in books, realizing we are not alone.

What makes written words literature rather than purely a mode of conveying information is not universally agreed – shopping lists and instruction manuals are not considered literature, but the borderline between practicality and poetry is hard to define. In this volume, we suggest that literature is anything written or spoken that tells a story, has a narrative, contains poetic or philosophical thought or tries in one way or another to convey a poetic, metaphoric or philosophical truth.

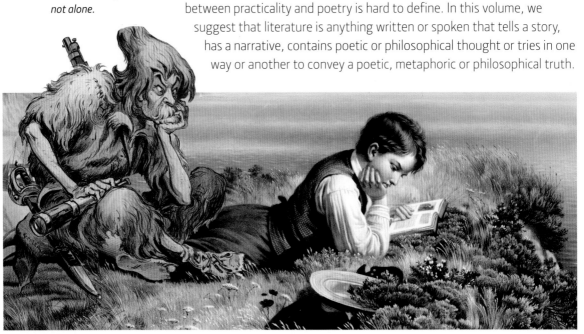

We have used the term to apply to spoken or sung texts too, including theatre and performance poetry.

It may seem strange to use the plural first-person pronoun when talking about reading, as literature for the most part is a pursuit we experience alone. Including the most intimate of artistic media, such as the poem and the novel, it still has the power to glue us together as a community of readers, as the growth of reading groups and websites like the hugely popular Goodreads have shown. The miracle of literature is that one imagination is able to speak to another through the conduit of the written word. Each work of literature is pregnant with infinite readings, and comes to readers at unique moments in their individual lives, with the particular experiences, thoughts and beliefs that each of us brings to bear. The words are the vessels that carry the imagination; once carved in stone, then on clay, wood, bamboo; then written on papyrus and tablets, then paper and now on screens. With their ever-evolving symbols and our ever-evolving lives, these words are open to continuous new interpretations.

This book gives an overview of the entire world of literature (as well as the literature of the world), from its origins even before the birth of writing, to the literature of the present and the future, too – though regrettably (but inevitably in a book that allows for 50 topics and no more) some forms have had to be omitted. Essays for instance do not appear; children's literature, travel literature and erotica are some of the forms that will have to be left for others to consider. Some literary movements have also been omitted for want of space, with Dadaism, Oulipo, The Black Arts Movement, Flarf and Alt Lit among many other topics we would like to have explored. Throughout this book, it has been our aim to include examples from as many literary cultures as we can, sometimes eschewing the most famous examples from the established literary canon.

Illustration has long been a valuable companion of literature and manga is one of its most successful modern manifestations.

Literature today is at an exciting point in history, accessible almost instantly to everyone, anywhere, and in the case of some books available in almost every known language. In an age where 'long form' writing is perhaps under threat from the immediate gratification of scattergun bursts of texts, snaps and tweets, this book aims to celebrate the deep satisfaction literature can offer in all its myriad, protean forms.

How this book works

Each topic is broken down to make it accessible. The 30-second thesis gives the main description, while the 3-second plot summarizes the topic at a glance. If you would like to find out more, the 3-minute theme examines an intriguing aspect of the topic and expands on it. The 3-second bibliographies list interesting texts of the period, genre or device for you to explore further.

The **History of Literature** gives an overview of literary endeavour through the ages. Then **The Novel** looks at one of the most popular forms of literature, which is considered through its many genres. **Literary Prose** examines short stories, autobiographies and memoirs, diaries, philosophical and religious works. **Poetry** explores the longest epic poems to the tiniest haikus. **Drama** surveys the uses we have made of the spoken word over millennia, using actors to explore the range of the human condition through plays that show us the extremes of fate. **Literary Devices** investigates the methods authors use to excite our imaginations and to intensify the effect of the work in the mind of the reader or listener. Finally, **Literary Styles** studies the different approaches to storytelling that grab the reader with playful, challenging or disturbing techniques, persuading them for the time it takes to read the book to suspend their disbelief and surrender to the vision that the writer has conjured in their minds.

HISTORY OF LITERATURE

HISTORY OF LITERATURE
GLOSSARY

alienation The state or experience of feeling alienated, a condition that informs much of modern literature, reflecting modern life since the Industrial Revolution, which entailed a loss of faith and of close-knit rural communities.

allegory A story, poem or work of drama that can be seen to have a hidden meaning, which is often religious or moral.

Aryan The name given to the Indo-European language speakers said to have migrated to India during the Vedic period of Indian history (ca. 1500–ca. 500 BCE).

bawdy Humorously indecent, referring to sexual matters.

Creole A language created by mixing two different languages, often one colonizing language and one colonized, particular to a specific region and born from a particular time in history when two cultures and languages melded together. Many creole languages exist in American and Indian Ocean colonies, as well as in Africa.

cuneiform An ancient system of writing developed by the Sumerians in 3500–3000 BCE. The word comes from the Latin *cuneus*, which means 'wedge'; the writing is wedge-shaped from the stylus cutting into the clay.

epic narrative or **verse** A long story, usually about heroic deeds, intense bravery or unusually impressive events.

fragmented narrative Fragmented narratives throw time into a kaleidoscope of jumbled moments, worked together by the writer in a way that challenges the reader to make sense of the story.

Gutenberg parenthesis The idea that the period in humanity's history during which text is of paramount importance is finite. Gutenberg invented the printing press between 1440 and 1450, and from that time until now writing has dominated human communication. People who subscribe to this idea believe that text will gradually be taken over by speech once more, with technology as an aid.

kāvya A term referring to a wide range of Sanskrit classical poetry, including both lyrical and epic poetry.

memoir An extended piece of writing about oneself, published for a general readership.

mnemonic devices Techniques to help people remember things, including rhymes, music, models and pictures. The Greeks would walk through the rooms of familiar buildings in their minds and attach memories to architectural features. This would enable them to revisit the imagined rooms and recall facts, passages of text, numbers and so on.

patois Informal speech, the dialect of a small geographical location, particularly one with low status comparative to the standard language of that country.

psalm A holy song or hymn, used in Christian and Jewish worship, originally set to music.

Romanticism (or **Romantics**) A movement in literature that originated in Europe in the late eighteenth century, flourishing from 1800 to 1850, which placed the individual at the heart of the work and emphasized imagination, our connection with nature and the overarching importance of emotion as paramount literary qualities.

Sanskrit The language of ancient India, one of the first Indo-Aryan languages and one of the oldest-known languages.

shruti A Sanskrit word meaning 'what is heard' that refers to the most ancient body of Hindu texts.

Sturm und Drang A literary movement of the late eighteenth century in Germany, in which extreme emotions and subjective opinions are given precedence over rationalism. Literally translated as 'Storm and Drive', it tends to be known as Storm and Stress in English.

temple hymns The Sumerian temple hymns were written on clay tablets around 2600 BCE and are considered the oldest literature in the world. The hymns addressed the temples themselves as if they were living beings.

Vedic Relating to the language used in the Vedas, a large body of Hindu texts; also an early form of Sanksrit.

Vorticism A short-lived literary and artistic movement founded by Wyndham Lewis – satirical novelist, polemicist and painter – which fetishized industrial modernity. A phenomenon lasting from 1912 to 1915, its place in modern cultural history is owed as much to the ground-breaking Vorticist magazine *Blast* as to the works of any one member.

THE ORAL TRADITION

the 30-second thesis

3-SECOND PLOT
The oral tradition is a form of knowledge transmitted from one generation to another, through speech and song, including folktales, verses, ballads, chants and epic narrative.

3-MINUTE THEME
Some academics suggest we are currently in a so-called Gutenberg Parenthesis, and that populations which at present are literate will gradually return to an oral tradition. This can easily be imagined, as developments in mobile technology see the younger generation recording voice messages and videos, while the use of keyboards and especially the pen are slowly being dropped – the written word eschewed in favour of an oral culture rooted in new technology.

Reading is a relatively recent development in human history, the first signs of literacy dating back a mere 6,000 years, while oral storytelling is entrenched in human consciousness. Literature evolved from oral histories handed down through successive generations, such as the Vedic chants of Hinduism. In some cases, not just the content but the style of delivery is preserved down to the inflections of voice as it is passed on from person to person. The retention techniques of the deliverers of these Vedic chants and their obsession with fidelity to the original, ensure that the work has remained virtually unchanged over hundreds of years. In less closely guarded oral literature, improvization is encouraged, to allow for individual interpretation and embellishments; and language is heightened for dramatic effect. Poets of the oral tradition use repetition, mnemonic devices, alliteration, assonance and proverbial sayings to aid memory. In recent years, spoken-word performance poetry and storytelling has become a global phenomenon, with performers such as Kate Tempest and Franny Choi revelling in their ability to provoke, subvert and recast social reality with the power of personal charisma. Spoken-word poetry is closely related to rap; as such it represents the voice of those who until now had been largely unrepresented in literature.

RELATED TOPICS
See also
EARLY LITERATURE
page 16

EPIC POEM
page 82

BALLAD
page 92

3-SECOND BIBLIOGRAPHY
THE ILIAD
ca. 762 BCE
Homer

GRIMM'S FAIRY TALES
1812
Jakob and Wilhelm Grimm

'WHAT I WILL'
2010
Suheir Hammad

'BONES'
2017
Titlope Sonuga

30-SECOND TEXT
Ella Berthoud

From the speeches of Cicero to the rhythm of rap, the spoken word compels us to stop what we're doing and listen.

EARLY LITERATURE

the 30-second thesis

Shrouded in the mystery that

surrounds ancient cultures, the earliest literature is in many cases uncertain in authorship and date. Many kinds of literature were explored by ancient writers, from epic narrative to spells designed to be read by the dead, and forms were unfixed for many centuries. Religious literature was one of the first examples of writing; the first people known to write were the Sumerians, around 2300 BCE, and the first named writer was Enheduanna, the high priestess of the gods Inanna and Nanna. In cuneiform script, she wrote temple hymns and intimate descriptions of her exile from and return to Ur. Separate from this sacred tradition, many ancient forms described battles; Mesopotamia's earliest known work was the bellicose *Epic of Gilgamesh*, circa 2100 BCE, written on clay. Literature that helped people to cross over into the afterlife was another early form, with one of the oldest examples known being the Egyptian *Book of the Dead* – or, more accurately, 'Spells for Going Forth by Day' – written initially on the walls of tombs and on amulets for the elite dead, as a manual for the afterlife placed with the body in the sarcophagus, and recorded eventually on the *Papyrus of Ani* around 1240–1250 BCE.

3-SECOND PLOT
Early literature refers to the very first writings known to humanity, including poems, epic tales and ballads, often written on stone, clay or papyrus.

3-MINUTE THEME
Philosophical writing was one of the earliest kinds of literature, appearing in different forms around the world. Laozi's *Tao Te Ching* (fifth century BCE), written in a series of verses, was originally inscribed on one-line bamboo strips tied together with silk thread, leaving its structure and meaning open to interpretation. Plato's Socratic dialogues (387–361 BCE), written in conversational form, became a popular format for philosophical discussions, emulated by philosophers as diverse as Denis Diderot, Jean-Francoise Revel and Iris Murdoch.

RELATED TOPICS
See also
SANSKRIT LITERATURE
page 18

RELIGIOUS TEXTS
page 76

EPIC POEM
page 82

3-SECOND BIBLIOGRAPHY
THE UPANISHADS
ca. 800–ca. 500 BCE

THEOGONY
ca. 700 BCE
Hesiod

THE ART OF WAR
ca. fifth century BCE
Sun Tzu

THE AENEID
ca. 30–ca. 18 BCE
Virgil

30-SECOND TEXT
Ella Berthoud

Some of the earliest writing has survived for thousands of years in the protected environments of Egyptian tombs.

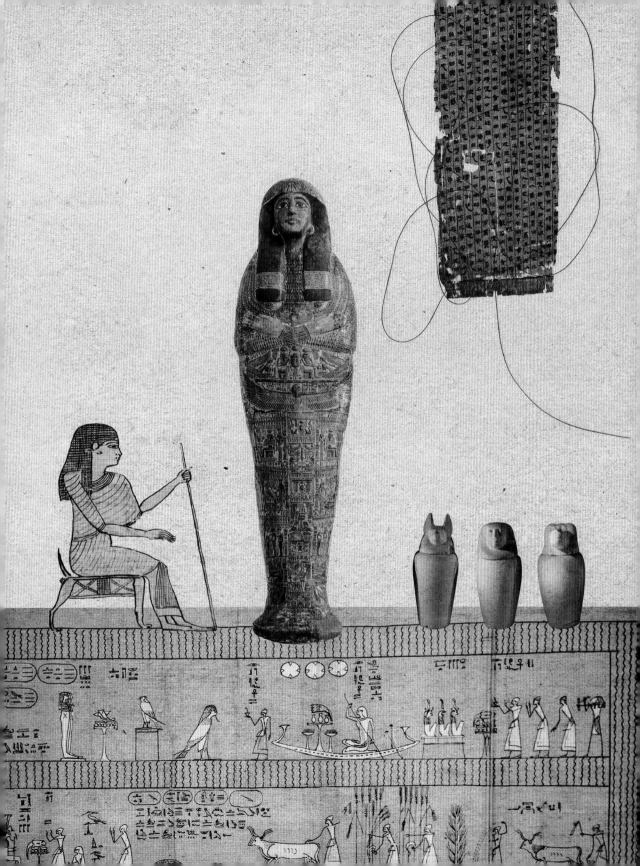

SANSKRIT LITERATURE

the 30-second thesis

3-SECOND PLOT
Sanskrit literature refers to texts written in the Sanskrit language since the second millennium BCE. It also includes modern literature written in Sanskrit.

3-MINUTE THEME
Sanskrit is not generally spoken as a living language today, but is used by Hindu priests in religious ceremonies and classified as one of the 22 official Indian languages. Modern Sanskrit writing is mainly done as an academic exercise, though there are still some writers composing poems in Sanskrit. One of the most famous modern Sanskrit authors is Satya Vrat Shastri who writes in various Sanskrit poetical forms, including the Mahākāvya, similar to the epic poem.

Sanskrit literature was transmitted orally, and for centuries before being written down was known as *shruti* or 'what is heard'. Sanskrit writings began around 1500 BCE with the era of the Vedic hymns, and its Classical era began around 500 BCE, overlapping the Vedic, and ended around 1000 CE. The word Sanskrit means 'perfected' and was a linguistic development of the Vedas, meaning knowledge. Sanskrit was the vehicle of expression for the much debated Aryan people who are believed to have arrived in the Indian subcontinent in 2000 BCE and gradually established themselves as the dominant cultural force in the region. Almost all Sanskrit literature is in verse, with some in dialogue form, beginning with the ten books of the Rig Veda Samhita (ca. 1200 BCE), the oldest Hindu religious text composed of 1,028 hymns, some of which are still used today in ceremonies such as weddings. Classical Sanskrit included a style of poetry known as *kāvya*, which was popularized by writers such as Ashvaghosa, a Brahman philosopher and poet who wrote the *Buddhacarita*, one of the most celebrated accounts of the life of the Buddha. Sanskrit drama, which flourished around 400 CE, is founded on the works of the fifth-century poet and dramatist Kālidāsa, who wrote a number of influential plays and poems that still resonate across the world.

RELATED TOPICS
See also
THE ORAL TRADITION
page 14

EARLY LITERATURE
page 16

RELIGIOUS TEXTS
page 76

3-SECOND BIBLIOGRAPHY
PANCHATANTRA
ca. 300 BCE

SVAPNAVĀSAVADATTĀ
ca. third century CE
Bhāsa

UTTARARĀMACARITA
700–730 CE
Bhavabhūti

NAISHADHACARITA
1174 CE
Śrīharṣa

30-SECOND TEXT
Ella Berthoud

Sanskrit verses are widely used in Hindu rituals, such as prayers from the Rig Veda at dawn and dusk.

EPIGASTRIC

चक्र - मणि पूरक.   दलोंकीभद्वल - डे सें फें तक.   देव - वृद्ध रुद्र.   ज्ञान कण्ड

न - नाम्रि.   नाम तत्त्व - अग्नि.   देवज्ञात्ति - डाकिनी.   संहार भाल न मं समर्थे और वचन नलने में चतुर
दल.   तत्त्वबीज - रं.   यंत्र - त्रिकोण   दो जाता है. और उसके जिह्वापर सरस्वती नि-
नील.   बीजका वाहन - मेष.   त्तम कर लेती है
                                                                        और श्री ज्ञान उन नाही बोध समूहक जिएहल्स

MEDIEVAL LITERATURE

the 30-second thesis

3-SECOND PLOT
Medieval literature was
that written from the fall
of Rome in 476 CE to the
late fifteenth century; it
includes both religious and
secular writing.

3-MINUTE THEME
In medieval times, authorial
ownership was considered
less important than faithful
rendition of the story.
Medieval authors were
inclined to embellish
classical stories with their
own digressions and
concoctions rather than
create something new.
The border between fiction
and non-fiction was far
less guarded than today;
authors frequently
declared historical
accuracy, even if long
passages of text were
invented, as in Geoffrey
of Monmouth's *The
History of the Kings
of Britain* (1100–55).

Medieval literature is usually associated with religious texts at a time when the Church dominated civic life, but the medieval period also saw the flourishing of profane literary works, such as Geoffrey Chaucer's 'The Miller's Tale' from *The Canterbury Tales* (ca. 1400), which is full of bawdy descriptions of sex. Nevertheless, across Europe, individually produced Books of Hours – devotional works for prayer and the recitation of psalms – highly illustrated and with full-page miniatures were widely owned among wealthier households, though out of reach for the rural poor. Illustration had been a part of literature since writing began but the medieval era was a time of lavish pictorial decoration. Popular forms in medieval literature included: epic poems such as *Beowulf* (ca. 1000), the oldest surviving work of Old English literature; religious and philosophical tracts such as Thomas Aquinas' *Summa Theologica* (ca. 1274); or travel memoirs like Marco Polo's *Book of the Marvels of the World* (ca. 1300). Another popular form involved the description of visions and dreams in the form of allegory, often told in the first person, such as *Pearl* (late fourteenth century), a Middle English poem by the same man who composed the chivalric romance *Gawain and the Green Knight* (late fourteenth century), whose story is still retold by modern poets today.

RELATED TOPICS
See also
RELIGIOUS TEXTS
page 76

EPIC POEM
page 82

ALLEGORY
page 122

3-SECOND BIBLIOGRAPHY
THE HERALD OF DIVINE LOVE
1289
Gertrude the Great

THE DIVINE COMEDY
1320
Dante Alighieri

THE LAND OF COCKAYGNE
ca. 1350
Anon

PIERS PLOWMAN
1365–90
William Langland

30-SECOND TEXT
Ella Berthoud

*While religious texts
were an important
aspect of medieval
literature, humour and
magic were also vital.*

EARLY MODERN LITERATURE

the 30-second thesis

3-SECOND PLOT
Early modern literature refers to European writing that coincided with the new scientific view of the world that emerged between the sixteenth and eighteenth centuries.

3-MINUTE THEME
Although the term 'early modern' in literature relates mostly to developments in Europe, elsewhere in the world writers experimented with different forms of love poetry. In Japan, Saikaku composed *The Great Mirror of Male Love* (1687) comprising 40 short stories describing homosexual love; and when his beloved wife died he composed a thousand-verse Hakai poem for her in just 12 hours. In Persia, Romantic verse was also in the ascendant, frequently extolling the love of young men.

Early modern literature covers the period between the sixteenth and eighteenth centuries, a time during which the science and technology of Europe established both new ways of understanding the material universe and the dominance of Europeans over increasingly large swathes of the non-European world. With the printed book now an established fact, the conditions existed for the emergence of popular narrative forms like the novel, which first emerged in this period, as well as the fairytale, a new kind of didactic folktale delivering salutary lessons for children, beginning with the tales of Charles Perrault published in 1697. But perhaps the dominant form of literature throughout the era was the stage play. Written for pure entertainment, this golden age of the theatre saw Shakespeare and Marlowe in England; Molière, Racine and Corneille in France; and Pedro Calderón de la Barca and Lope de Vega in Spain establish a body of plays that remain the core repertoire of the modern theatre. Epic poetry such as John Milton's *Paradise Lost* (1667) tackled both religious themes and social satire, while overtly satirical prose works, such as Jonathan Swift's *Gulliver's Travels* (1726), poked fun at other works or literary genres, assuming that an increasingly literate public would get the joke.

RELATED TOPICS
See also
THE BIRTH OF THE NOVEL
page 36

EPIC POEM
page 82

SATIRE
page 144

3-SECOND BIBLIOGRAPHY
DR FAUSTUS
ca. 1589–92
Christopher Marlowe

TARTUFFE
1664
Molière

OROONOKO
1688
Aphra Behn

TALES AND STORIES OF THE PAST WITH MORALS
1695
Charles Perrault

30-SECOND TEXT
Ella Berthoud

Despite the increasing spread of literacy, theatre was the most popular literary form throughout this period.

MODERN LITERATURE

the 30-second thesis

3-SECOND PLOT
Modern literature refers to literature written from the late eighteenth century to the twenty-first. From romanticism to realism to radicalism, modern literature has evolved dramatically.

3-MINUTE THEME
Children's literature had not been a genre in its own right until the modern age, as fairytales were written as much for adults as for children. It became a publishing phenomenon in the mid-nineteenth century with the emergence of a new, more liberal attitude to childhood, an increase in the educated middle classes, and the development of colour printing. John Newbury's *A Little Pretty Pocket-Book* (1744) is now widely considered the first modern children's book.

In late-eighteenth century

Europe, the *Sturm und Drang* movement inspired Goethe to write *The Sorrows of Young Werther*, which became a crucial influence on the Romantics. In Britain, at the dawn of the Industrial Revolution, English Romantics such as William Wordsworth and John Keats reacted to the mechanization of agriculture and the inhuman conditions of the textile industry, as people moved away from the countryside into cities, by memorializing the pastoral England being left behind and seeking a transcendental alternative to the present. A more visionary approach was taken by William Blake, whose prophetic poetry criticized slavery and child labour. Realism (and later Naturalism), which emerged in the mid-nineteenth century, attempted to portray everyday life and rejected Romanticism, beginning in France with Honoré de Balzac and Stendhal, and spreading through Europe and America for the rest of the century and beyond through the work of authors such as Charles Dickens, George Eliot, Émile Zola and Henry James. The realist impulse in Russian literature gave rise to a new level of psychological depth in the novels, plays and stories of Leo Tolstoy, Anton Chekhov and Fyodor Dostoevsky, which in turn provided the ground for the Modernist revolution that followed in the early twentieth century.

RELATED TOPICS
See also
MODERNIST LITERATURE
page 28

REALISM
page 140

3-SECOND BIBLIOGRAPHY
SONGS OF INNOCENCE AND OF EXPERIENCE
1794
William Blake

DEAD SOULS
1842
Nikolay Gogol

JANE EYRE
1847
Charlotte Brontë

THE HOUSE OF MIRTH
1905
Edith Wharton

30-SECOND TEXT
Ella Berthoud

William Wordsworth was a key voice in the Romantic movement, which emerged during the Industrial Revolution.

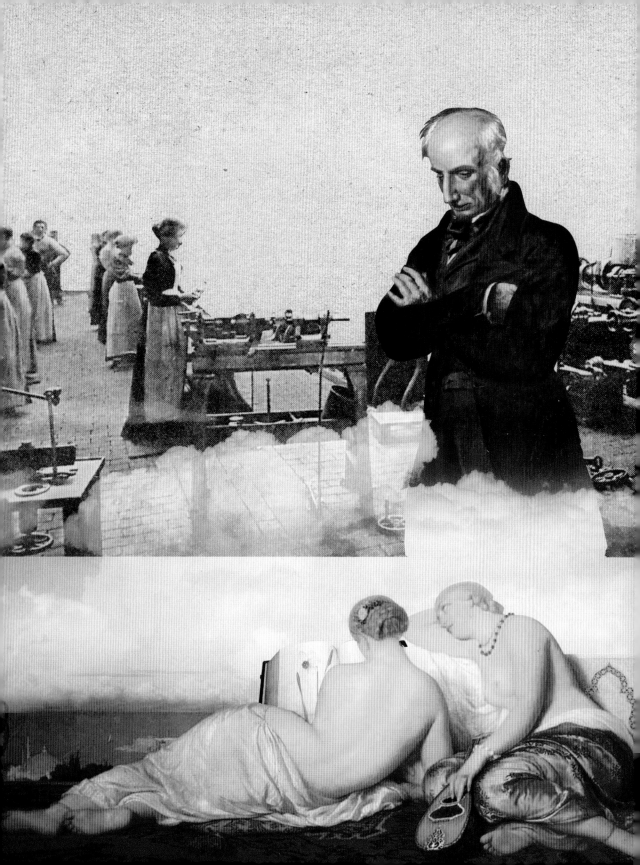

10 September 1886
Born in Bethlehem,
Pennsylvania

1911
Moves to London

1913
Marries Richard Aldington

1916–17
Literary editor of *Egoist*
journal

1917
Becomes involved with
D.H. Lawrence

1918
Moves in with Cecil Gray

ca. 1918
Becomes involved with
Bryher (Annie Winifred
Ellerman)

1919
Daughter Frances Perdita
Aldington born

1921
Writes *Paint it Today*
(novel), not published
until 1992

1921–22
Writes *Asphodel* (novel)

1926
Palimpsest (novel)
published

1928
Hedylus (novel) published

1946
Moves to Switzerland
after suffering a mental
breakdown

1952–54
Helen in Egypt (poetry
collection) published

1960
The Gift (memoir)
published

1960
First woman to receive
Poetry medal from the
American Academy of
Arts and Letters

27 September 1961
Suffers a stroke in Zurich
and dies

HILDA DOOLITTLE

Born in 1886, Hilda Doolittle was a poet, novelist and memoirist of the first half of the twentieth century, who was largely forgotten until the explosion of women's poetry and culture in the 1970s brought a new, avid audience to her work.

She was born in Bethlehem, Pennsylvania, her mother an artist and musician, and her father an astronomer who disapproved of her artistic aspirations. At fifteen, Hilda met Ezra Pound and then William Carlos Williams; ten years later, in 1911, she followed them to Europe. In London, Pound worked with her on her poetry, appending the word '*Imagiste*' to her work, a label that would stick with her for the rest of her life. In the summer of 1912 she, Pound and the poet Richard Aldington declared themselves 'the three Imagists'. Their principles were to use no word that did not contribute directly to the work; to directly treat the 'thing', whether subjective or objective; and 'to compose in the sequence of the musical phrase, not in the sequence of the metronome'.

At first she swore never to marry and was openly bisexual, taking a series of lovers. But in 1913 she married Aldington and they moved to Cornwall, though they were later estranged.

Her first book, *Sea Garden*, was published in 1916. Three years later, Doolittle conceived a child, Perdita, with Cecil Gray, a composer and friend of D.H. Lawrence, but by the time the child was born the relationship had ended and Hilda had met Bryher, a female novelist from a wealthy family, who became her lover, financial supporter and co-parent. Doolittle and Bryher travelled to Greece in 1919 where together they experienced profound shared hallucinations. Doolittle (or H.D., as she became known) later spoke of what Bryher called the 'jelly-fish' experience of having a double ego – she (Doolittle) felt she had a bell-jar or hemisphere of glass, like a diving bell, around her head, with another appearing from her feet and encasing the first. This intense experience formed the catalyst for H.D.'s *Notes on Thought and Vision*, now considered a classic of feminist prose.

H.D. spent the rest of her life writing poetry, novels, and her greatest work, *Helen in Egypt*, a uniquely personal account of Helen of Troy's inner life during the aftermath of the Trojan War, written in epic form and weaving the raw material of her own life into the bones of a cultural myth. She died in 1961.

Ella Berthoud

MODERNIST LITERATURE

the 30-second thesis

3-SECOND PLOT
Modernist literature experiments with form – using stream of consciousness and fragmented narratives – and critiquing its host culture's traditional values, sometimes through a first-person narrator.

3-MINUTE THEME
Modernists Wyndham Lewis and Ezra Pound postulated in their Vorticist magazine *Blast* (1914) that there is no such thing as absolute truth, that all things are relative and that the individual is sovereign. They inferred that the world is created in the act of perceiving it, and that the individual's view is paramount. Hence narrative authority was now found in the voice of the protagonist rather than the illusory conceit of an omniscient narrator.

Modernist literature emerged from the horror of the First World War. A sense of despair, loss and alienation from all that had gone before made discontinuity with the past the most meaningful literary response to a present revealed to be godless, chaotic and brutal, with Modernist writing characterized by disruptions to the integrity of character, place and time that were the bedrock of nineteenth-century Realism. This feeling of abandonment, confusion and uncertainty is perfectly portrayed in Wilfred Owen's 'Anthem for Doomed Youth' (1917). Like Modernist novels of the period, the fragmented forms of Modernist poems such as T.S. Eliot's *The Waste Land* (1922) reflected not only a loss of faith in traditional belief systems but also a new understanding of the influence of the unconscious mind on conscious actions, as examined in the work of Sigmund Freud. The new psychological complexity was expressed in the stream-of-consciousness narratives of William Faulkner's *As I Lay Dying* (1930) and Virginia Woolf's *Mrs Dalloway* (1925), among other novels, as was a broken sense of historical continuity, with elements of mythology and ancient literary history underpinning the structure and disturbing the surface of those works of Joyce and Eliot, often through direct fragmentary quotations from ancient text, like rents in the fabric of time.

RELATED TOPICS
See also
FREE VERSE
page 84

NARRATIVE VOICE
page 138

STREAM OF CONSCIOUSNESS
page 150

3-SECOND BIBLIOGRAPHY
THE CANTOS
1915–62
Ezra Pound

THE TRIAL
1925
Franz Kafka

TRILOGY: MOLLOY, MALONE DIES, THE UNNAMEBLE
1951–55
Samuel Beckett

BID ME TO LIVE
1960
Hilda Doolittle

30-SECOND TEXT
Ella Berthoud

After the monumental and pointless loss of life in the First World War, authors turned to fragmented narratives.

POSTCOLONIAL LITERATURE

the 30-second thesis

3-SECOND PLOT
Postcolonial literature refers to literary works written since decolonization in the 1950s and 1960s by writers from countries once colonized by former European empires.

3-MINUTE THEME
Colonial literature written by Europeans, such as Rudyard Kipling's poem 'The White Man's Burden' (1899), often traded in crude racial attitudes – portraying the colonized as inferior to the colonizers – that were vital to maintaining the illusion of the legitimacy of colonialism. Postcolonial literature gives the colonized the voice denied to them, often in an amended version of the former colonial language, to emphasize the message of self-determination to oppressor and oppressed alike.

Postcolonial literature is a term applied to work by non-European writers in continents whose nations were once colonies of European empires, implying that these works have been shaped primarily by the experience or historical legacy of colonialism. This is certainly the case in novels by black African writers, such as Kenyan author Ngũgĩ wa Thiong'o's *Devil on the Cross* (1980), which investigates the social malaise inherited from colonization and its concomitant capitalism, though the term applies equally to white, settler writers in former colonies, such as J.M. Coetzee, whose novel *Disgrace* (1999) explores the postcolonial trauma of a brutalized, post-apartheid South Africa. Like all such labels, 'postcolonial' is both an historical fact – the narrator of Salman Rushdie's magical-realist novel *Midnight's Children* (1981), for instance, is born at the moment of India's independence in 1947 – and an umbrella term that encompasses a huge variety of writers and writing and a much wider frame of cultural reference than is implied by the term. St Lucian writer Derek Walcott's epic poem *Omeros* (1990), for example, retells Homer's *The Iliad* in a Caribbean setting, frequently using patois and Creole language, and appropriates the ancient European story in a cultural echo of the original process of colonization itself.

RELATED TOPICS
See also
SHORT STORY
page 66

NARRATIVE VOICE
page 138

SATIRE
page 144

3-SECOND BIBLIOGRAPHY
THINGS FALL APART
1958
Chinua Achebe

SEASON OF MIGRATION TO THE NORTH
1966
Tayeb Salih

A SMALL PLACE
1988
Jamaica Kincaid

A FINE BALANCE
1995
Rohinton Mistry

30-SECOND TEXT
Ella Berthoud

With the end of colonial rule, postcolonial writers could reclaim their histories and create new futures.

THE NOVEL

THE NOVEL
GLOSSARY

bildungsroman Novels whose central focus is a protagonist's psychological and moral growth through youth and education into adulthood.

bodice ripper A sexually explicit romantic novel, a genre known today as erotic fiction.

flintlock A subgenre of fantasy fiction using the technology and aesthetic ideals of the early Industrial Revolution. The term refers to the striking mechanism of a gun that uses a flint in the hammer to strike a spark.

folklore Traditional stories and beliefs passed down by word of mouth, different in every culture and in many cases dating back to preliterate times. Folklore is always particular to the geographical region in which it is the local narrative tradition, its body of stories referring to indigenous plants, rituals and customs as well as cultural figures.

grimdark Characterized by violent, dystopian and bleak subject matter, a subgenre of fantasy fiction that sets out to disturb.

monologic/dialogic/polylogic Texts written in one voice are monologic; those in two voices are dialogic; those in three or more voices are polylogic.

mytho-fantasy A genre combining mythological and fantastical themes, particularly popular in India, but also significantly in Africa and China, and with many variations worldwide.

mythology From the ancient Greek word *mythos* meaning speech, fiction, narrative or plot. Mythology is a collection of stories and tales, often involving divine beings, from a single culture or religion. Gods, demigods, humans with unusual powers and creation stories are all typically part of a region's mythology.

novella A narrative piece of prose fiction that is longer than a short story but shorter than a novel, typically between 17,000 words and 40,000 words, deriving from the Italian word *novella* (the feminine of *novello*), meaning 'new'.

pansexual Those who are gender-blind and fall in love with people regardless of their sex and sexuality.

progenitor An ancestor or parent, or a person who sets in motion an artistic, literary, intellectual or other cultural movement.

pulp fiction Popular fiction written in the first half of the twentieth century for cheaply produced periodicals known as 'pulps', as opposed to glossy magazines, known as 'slicks'. The word 'pulp' refers to the coarse wood pulp from which they were made. The term came to be associated with the lurid subject matter of the stories, being either gory or sexually explicit.

romance In popular fiction, romance novels are those based around love between men and women. Generally this type of fiction is light and mass-market in tone.

Spanish Inquisition An organization within the Roman Catholic Church created to discover and punish people whose religious beliefs differed from their own, characterized by torture and extreme violence. In existence from 1478 to 1834, many of its victims were executed.

speculative fiction Fiction in which the author looks to the future at possible directions in which humanity might go. Potentially involving horror, fantasy, futurism and historical overlaps, its key characteristic is in asking the question 'What if?'

steampunk A subgenre of fantasy fiction that creates fantastical worlds with the attitudes, settings and aesthetics of Victorian era Britain and technology inspired by nineteenth-century steam-powered machinery.

Webtoons A type of digital comic published exclusively online, originating in South Korea. These are now read on smartphones and as a result have reached an equal level of readership with comics published offline in the same country; print sales have declined while digital sales have increased.

zeitgeist The defining spirit or mood of a particular period of history, encapsulated in its prevailing ideas, beliefs and mood.

THE BIRTH
OF THE NOVEL

the 30-second thesis

Long fictional narratives

describing human experiences on an intimate psychological basis, the first works now regarded as novels emerged in Japan, with Murasaki Shikibu's *Tale of Genji* (ca. 1010) and China, with novels such as Shi Nai'an's *Water Margin* (fourteenth century). The progenitors of the European novel included epic verse narratives, such as Geoffrey Chaucer's *Canterbury Tales* (fourteenth century), and spiritual autobiographies, such as that of Saint Teresa of Ávila (1565), with their intense focus on the inner life of the narrator. Verse epics gradually gave way to prose as authors saw the benefits of combining popular stories, previously written in verse, with serious histories, composed in prose, the historical elements bringing an educational quality to what would otherwise be a mere entertainment. Because of their length, novels were the first form of literature that allowed space for in-depth character development, rather than simply being a record of their deeds. The English word 'novel' derives from the Italian *novella*, meaning a short story about 'something new'. At first there was some debate as to whether novels were the same as romances; Cervantes's *Don Quixote* (1615), frequently cited as the first modern novel, was shaped by that debate.

3-SECOND PLOT
The earliest form to be concerned with the inner life of a character, the novel's elastic length allows scope for the character's development over time.

3-MINUTE THEME
In the tenth century, ceramic movable characters developed in China for printing allowed for the development of the novel in that region. In Europe it was not until 1450 that Johannes Gutenberg developed movable individual letter blocks for roman script, allowing mass production of printed material. Initially, large sheets of printed and folded paper, known as chapbooks, sold in millions across Europe, but their popularity would later be eclipsed by the novel.

RELATED TOPICS
See also
EARLY LITERATURE
page 16

MEDIEVAL LITERATURE
page 20

EPIC POEM
page 82

3-SECOND BIBLIOGRAPHY
THE GOLDEN ASS
ca. 150 CE
Lucius Apuleius

ROMANCE OF THE THREE KINGDOMS
fourteenth century
Luo Guanzhong

ROBINSON CRUSOE
1719
Daniel Defoe

TRISTRAM SHANDY
1759
Laurence Sterne

30-SECOND TEXT
Ella Berthoud

Gutenberg's invention of movable type paved the way for novels like **Robinson Crusoe** *to be read globally.*

EPISTOLARY NOVEL

the 30-second thesis

3-SECOND PLOT
An epistolary novel is
one in which the narrative
is largely revealed in letters
between two or more
characters or from one
to another.

3-MINUTE THEME
Modern epistolary
novels allow for unreliable
narrators to share their
intimate thoughts, leaving
the reader to guess who is
telling the truth, as in
Lionel Shriver's *We Need
to Talk about Kevin* (2003);
and to show us the inner
workings of a mind in a way
that could not be revealed
in linear and conventional
narrative, such as in
Marilynne Robinson's
Pulitzer Prize-winning
novel *Gilead* (2004).

A novel written in the form of
letters allows for the expression of multiple
intimate viewpoints without interference from
an authorial voice. One of the first kinds of
novel, the epistolary form emerged from the
universal habit of writing letters, with *Prison of
Love* (ca. 1485) by Diego de San Pedro, in which
a large number of letters create much of the
intensely romantic narrative, being the earliest-
known example of the form. Epistolary novels
are of three basic types: monologic, where
the letters are all from one person, such as
Marilynne Robinson's *Gilead* (2004); dialogic,
with letters between two people, such as
Helene Hanff's *84, Charing Cross Road* (1970);
and polylogic, with three or more letter-writing
characters, as in Bram Stoker's *Dracula* (1897).
In the eighteenth century, the form was
lampooned for its heavy moralizing content,
notably with Henry Fielding's *Shamela* (1741),
a parody of Samuel Richardson's widely read
Pamela (1740), in which the narrator is found
scribbling letters under the most ridiculous
circumstances; such mockery did not diminish
the popularity of similar novels of the time.
More recently, authors have seized on email,
text and Post-it notes as rich new formats for
epistolary exchange, as in Maria Semple's
Where'd You Go, Bernadette (2012).

RELATED TOPICS
See also
THE BIRTH OF THE NOVEL
page 36

ROMANCE
page 54

NARRATIVE VOICE
page 138

3-SECOND BIBLIOGRAPHY
THE COLOR PURPLE
1982
Alice Walker

BLACK BOX
1986
Amos Oz

THE HISTORIAN
2005
Elizabeth Kostova

THE WHITE TIGER
2008
Aravind Adiga

30-SECOND TEXT
Ella Berthoud

*Fictionalized private
thoughts addressed
to others in letters
have long been a
popular literary form
with readers.*

HISTORICAL NOVEL

the 30-second thesis

3-SECOND PLOT
Historical novels tell a tale from another era, bringing it to life for the present day.

3-MINUTE THEME
Children are often introduced to history via the historical novel, for instance, seventeenth-century France in Alexandre Dumas's *The Three Musketeers* (1844), the English Civil War in Frederick Marryat's *The Children of the New Forest* (1847) or the Nazi occupation of Denmark in Lois Lowry's *Number the Stars* (1989). By taking them back and revealing the lives of those who preceded us, children can develop empathy with other times and cultures.

As a rule, an historical novel should be set at least 50 years before it was written. The world's earliest literature was frequently based on historical episodes, having evolved from oral histories of real and mythical events. Historical novels revel in their fidelity to details of manners, social conditions and notable figures of the past. They have been popular since the time of Sir Walter Scott and his *Waverley* novels (1814–24) and today include works examining recent events which, though breaking the 50-year rule, are also regarded as historical. Complete fidelity to real events is not always paramount; many historical novels weave in fictional elements to complement the verifiable historical facts, attributing imagined words and thoughts to characters who may or may not be historical figures, such as the fictional Don Fabrizio in Giuseppe Tomasi di Lampedusa's *The Leopard* (1958), through whose vivid inner life we view the *Risorgimento* of mid-nineteenth century Italy. Another narrative tactic can be seen in Hilary Mantel's novel *Wolf Hall* (2009), which plunges us into the Tudor period through its use of the historic present tense, a storytelling convention that lends a sense of immediacy. As with forward-looking fiction, for authors writing historical fiction, the present is their cornerstone.

RELATED TOPICS
See also
NARRATIVE VOICE
page 138

THE ORAL TRADITION
page 14

POSTCOLONIAL LITERATURE
page 30

3-SECOND BIBLIOGRAPHY
WATER MARGIN
ca. 1589
Shi Nai'an

WAR AND PEACE
1869
Leo Tolstoy

THE RED TENT
1997
Anita Diamant

THE GLASS PALACE
2000
Amitav Ghosh

30-SECOND TEXT
Ella Berthoud

Works by Alexandre Dumas and Sir Walter Scott are still among the most widely read historical novels.

SCIENCE FICTION

the 30-second thesis

3-SECOND PLOT
Science fiction is a genre in which the author can predict and even influence the future.

3-MINUTE THEME
Science fiction has often been dismissed by the literary establishment as it is closely associated with pulp fiction and low-budget movies. However, many of the greatest literary writers, from Mary Shelley to Kazuo Ishiguro have written sci-fi, and some of the most challenging literary works come in this form, using the dramatic potential of the future to ask fundamental questions about the human condition: where do we come from, what are we and where are we going?

In science fiction more than any other genre, the author can be seen as a prophet, though in 1959 the classic American sci-fi writer Robert A. Heinlein described the form, more modestly, as 'Realistic speculation about possible future events'. Some authors insist the genre should be firmly based in modern science and technology, while others, such as Margaret Atwood suggest the term 'speculative fiction' is more appropriate. The Sumerian *Epic of Gilgamesh*, written around 2100 BCE, could be regarded as the first work of science fiction, with themes such as the search for immortality that are still common in sci-fi today. The rise of the nineteenth-century novel coincided with great scientific leaps, giving writers such as Jules Verne, H.G. Wells and Begum Rokeya a chance to explore science, politics and moral issues in full-length works. Sci-fi short stories, such as those of Philip K. Dick, have also been popular, with some being turned into Hollywood films. Contemporary science fiction is complex and multilayered, as in multi-volume sagas such as *Quicksilver (The Baroque Cycle)* by Neal Stephenson (2003), while in Africa and India sci-fi writing is closely connected with the popular subgenre of mytho-fantasy.

RELATED TOPICS
See also
UTOPIA/DYSTOPIA
page 50

FANTASY
page 52

SHORT STORY
page 66

3-SECOND BIBLIOGRAPHY
WE
1920
Yevgeny Zamyatin

2001: A SPACE ODYSSEY
1968
Arthur C. Clarke

ANT LIFE
2007
Wang Jinkang

ZOO CITY
2010
Lauren Beukes

30-SECOND TEXT
Ella Berthoud

In depicting the future, sci-fi writers extrapolate from the most modern technology, though such stories can also date rapidly.

CRIME

the 30-second thesis

In crime fiction authors explore
the motives of criminals, their crimes and
possible retribution. Crime storytelling goes
back to the Song Dynasty (960–1279) in China
when tales of government magistrates solving
criminal cases were conveyed through oral
storytelling and puppetry. Though he may
not have been the first, Edgar Allan Poe is
widely credited with creating detective fiction
(a subgenre of crime) as it is known today,
through stories such as 'The Murders in the
Rue Morgue' (1841), featuring C. Auguste Dupin,
the first eccentric detective. In this character
Poe combined the uncanny intellect of the
detective with a scientific detachment that
became typical of fictional crime-solvers
thereafter, such as Arthur Conan Doyle's
Sherlock Holmes. Conan Doyle is credited with
the remarkable popularity of 'locked-room
mysteries', in which no perpetrator could
seemingly have left or entered the crime
scene. This detective subgenre thrived from
the 1840s to the 1950s through writers such
as Agatha Christie and Akimitsu Takagi. Today,
crime subgenres like Scandi noir, such as Stieg
Larsson's *Millennium* trilogy (2005–07),
courtroom dramas like Scott Turow's *Presumed
Innocent* (1987) and forensic thrillers such as
Patricia Cornwell's *Body Farm* (1994), have kept
readers up all night with their doors locked.

3-SECOND PLOT
A crime novel is one in
which the laws of soceity
are broken, the perpetrator
is investigated and the
crime is explored.

3-MINUTE THEME
During the 1850s,
translated versions of
Poe's short stories and
their spin-offs were
published cheaply in Italy
with yellow covers; these
immensely popular works
became known as *libri gialli*
(yellow books). To this day
crime novels are called
gialli in Italy. Gradually,
an Italian elite emerged
who subverted the genre,
deliberately leaving crimes
unsolved and the reader
hanging. Umberto Eco,
Carlo Emilio Gadda and
Leonardo Sciascia were
some of the greatest
exponents of the genre.

RELATED TOPICS
See also
HORROR
page 48

FANTASY
page 52

3-SECOND BIBLIOGRAPHY
PIETR LE LETTON
1931
Georges Simenon

DEAD WATER
1964
Ngaio Marsh

DEATH OF A RED HEROINE
2000
Qui Xiaolong

SACRED GAMES
2006
Vikram Chandra

30-SECOND TEXT
Ella Berthoud

*Fingerprints and
forensics are integral
to many crime novels,
as are wronged
innocents whose
stories must be told.*

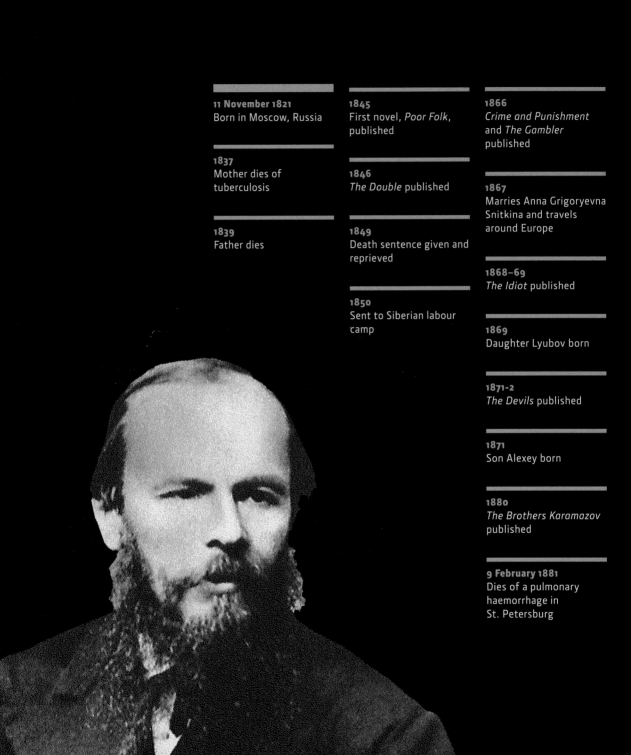

11 November 1821
Born in Moscow, Russia

1837
Mother dies of
tuberculosis

1839
Father dies

1845
First novel, *Poor Folk*,
published

1846
The Double published

1849
Death sentence given and
reprieved

1850
Sent to Siberian labour
camp

1866
Crime and Punishment
and *The Gambler*
published

1867
Marries Anna Grigoryevna
Snitkina and travels
around Europe

1868–69
The Idiot published

1869
Daughter Lyubov born

1871-2
The Devils published

1871
Son Alexey born

1880
The Brothers Karamazov
published

9 February 1881
Dies of a pulmonary
haemorrhage in
St. Petersburg

FYODOR DOSTOEVSKY

Dostoevsky has been described as the greatest psychologist the world of literature has ever known. He was born in 1821 in Moscow, where he lived with his parents and siblings in the grounds of a hospital for the poor. His imagination was sparked by his nanny, Alena Frolovna, who read him fairytales, Greek epics and heroic tales by Cervantes and Sir Walter Scott, as well as Russian classics.

When Fyodor was 15, his mother died of tuberculosis and he was sent to a Military Engineering Institute to prepare for a life in the army. The young man's bearing was markedly unmilitary, and although he was brave he was known mostly for his religious fervour, for which he was given the nickname of Monk Photius. He had always been aware of having what he called a 'nervous condition', which revealed itself as epilepsy when his father died suddenly in 1839 and Fyodor had his first fit; the novelist later described having more than one hundred such fits over his lifetime, and four characters in his novels have epilepsy, Prince Myshkin in *The Idiot* (1868–69) being the most powerfully drawn. Indeed, Dostoevsky's descriptions of his seizures contributed to medical understanding of the condition, with his particular ailment, known as 'ecstatic epilepsy', being preceded by what he described as a happiness unimaginable to others – an experience quite impossible in an ordinary state.

He published his first novel, *Poor Folk*, in 1845, to critical acclaim, though his next, *The Double* (1846), was a failure at the time. He developed a gambling addiction, and fell in with a group of intellectual socialists, the Petrashevsky Circle. In 1849 he was denounced for 'anti-government' activities, and was sentenced to death along with five other people. At the last minute he was pardoned, but was sentenced instead to four years' hard labour in Siberia, where he lived among 'fleas, lice and black beetles', with his hands and feet shackled. This experience formed the basis for *The House of the Dead* (1861).

Soon after his release he married Maria Dimitrievna, a widow who later died in 1864. In 1867 he married Anna Snitkina, with whom he lived in St Petersburg and had four children, two of whom died very young. *The Brothers Karamazov* (1880), his final masterpiece, was published a year before he died from a pulmonary haemorrhage. By then a towering figure in Russian letters, he was mourned by thousands.

Ella Berthoud

HORROR

the 30-second thesis

Intended to shock, scare,

frighten and repel, horror has its roots in many cultures; from the vampire-like entity Emikku in ancient Sumerian literature, who inhabited the bodies of those who had died violent deaths, giving us the seeds of vampirism, to the Spanish Inquisition whose obsession with witchcraft gave rise to the first horror novels in European literature, with themes of religious intolerance and ritual execution. Robert Louis Stevenson's *Dr Jekyll and Mr Hyde* (1886) explored the theme of the remorseless psychopath at large in society; the book spawned a subgenre of horror (psychopathy) that thrives to this day. Modern horror fiction often portrays a character suffering a personal trauma or deteriorating mental health, as in Stephen King's *The Shining* (1977), in which an alcoholic descends into madness in an empty hotel. Strange houses and architectural anomalies such as a home being larger on the inside than the outside or having a bottomless basement provide fodder for stories such as Mark Danielewski's *House of Leaves* (2000) in which the house itself seems malevolent. The evil forces in horror fiction are often metaphors for the fears of contemporary society in the same way as science fiction explores our fears for the future.

RELATED TOPICS
See also
CRIME
page 44

FANTASY
page 52

GOTHIC
page 146

3-SECOND PLOT
Horror novels tell gruesome, macabre and shocking tales that frighten and thrill, terrifying and reassuring us at the same time.

3-MINUTE THEME
Contemporary horror novels explore themes that are common to films, such as malevolent forces that lurk behind our digital screens. The novel *Ring* (1991), by Koji Suzuki, also a film, investigates a virus that attacks viewers of a video, while *Pulse* (2001), by Kurosawa Kyoshi, has characters vanishing after meeting ghosts on their computers. *Friend Request* (2017), by Laura Marshall, focuses on the evils of social media, now a major theme in all literary genres.

3-SECOND BIBLIOGRAPHY
THE BLACK SPIDER
1842
Jeremias Gotthelf

'THE CALL OF CTHULHU'
1926
H.P. Lovecraft

AMERICAN PSYCHO
1991
Brett Easton Ellis

MY SOUL TO KEEP
1997
Tananarive Due

30-SECOND TEXT
Ella Berthoud

Writers like Stephen King were too scared by their own stories to publish them at first; readers beware!

UTOPIA/DYSTOPIA

the 30-second thesis

3-SECOND PLOT

Utopias are idealized places where everything is perfect. Dystopias are dehumanized societies, suggesting the fate of our own if contemporary warnings go unheeded.

3-MINUTE THEME

The term 'utopia', as used by Sir Thomas More for the title of his 1516 novel, comes from the Greek meaning 'no place', suggesting a non-existent society. The more recent, and homophonic, 'eutopia' comes from the Greek for 'good place', denoting a positive society. Literary dystopias are more common, however, perhaps showing that society's fears for the future outweigh the prospect of any paradise we might hope to see.

Though utopian societies had been described before 1516 – for example, Plato's *Republic* (ca. 380 BCE) – the tradition of utopian fiction, which depicts a perfect society, began with a single novel, Sir Thomas More's *Utopia* (1516), from which the genre gets its name. In More's visionary book, property and food are equally distributed, there is a welfare state, people learn agriculture and an essential trade, and there is no engagement with war. Though often unrealistic and impractical – one person's utopia is another's dystopia – utopias are nonetheless a means of exploring the possibility of fundamental social change, as for example in *Herland* (1915) by Charlotte Perkins Gilman, which depicts a society run by women. Dystopias, conversely, depict nightmare futures in which current social evils are exaggerated to the extent that society is destroyed, in many cases leaving the protagonist to fight for survival in a desolate country, as in Cormac McCarthy's *The Road* (2006). In some dystopias, such as *The Handmaid's Tale* (1985) by Margaret Atwood, a tyrannical leader segregates and oppresses sections of that society, creating a rigid hierarchy maintained by violence. Common themes in dystopias include politics, economics, family, feminism, religion, identity, violence, ecological destruction, science and technology.

RELATED TOPIC

See also
SCIENCE FICTION
page 42

3-SECOND BIBLIOGRAPHY

EREWHON
1872
Samuel Butler

NEWS FROM NOWHERE
1890
William Morris

SULTANA'S DREAM
1905
Rokeya Sakhawat Hossain

UTOPIA
2008
Ahmed Khaled Tawfik

THE POWER
2016
Naomi Alderman

BEFORE SHE SLEEPS
2018
Bina Shah

30-SECOND TEXT
Naomi Frisby

It is easier to imagine a bleak future than a bright one; hence the greater number of dystopian stories.

FANTASY

the 30-second thesis

3-SECOND PLOT
In fantasy fiction the imaginary world can be completely invented, bearing no relation to the real world.

3-MINUTE THEME
Magic Realism is a close cousin of fantasy, with elements of magic seeping into real situations, though in these instances the magic is a small element in an otherwise realistic world. The fantastical elements in Magic Realism are often not regarded by the characters as anything unusual, but accepted unquestioningly as part of life, as in Gabriel García Márquez's *One Hundred Years of Solitude* (1967) when Remedios the Beauty floats up to heaven.

Fantasy draws on folklore and mythology for inspiration. It allows readers to escape from the everyday world into one where magic exists, while authors can explore a limitless world of fairies, dragons and mythical creatures, where humans can fly, cheat death or change form. Two Roman texts, Ovid's *Metamorphoses* (8 CE) and Apuleius's *The Golden Ass* (ca. 150 CE), in which humans change into animals and trees, have exerted a major influence on the genre. Fantasy novels are often set in medieval times, a period which, preceding industrialization and scientific discovery, affords imaginative licence for dragons, witches and magic. It was one famous late Victorian medievalist, William Morris, who created the modern genre with books like *The Well at the World's End* (1896). In the 1920s, fantasy also entered the popular consciousness in the USA and Europe with magazines such as *Weird Tales*, while in the mid-twentieth century J.R.R. Tolkien's Middle Earth became a global phenomenon. Since then, fantasy literature – including subgenres like grimdark, flintlock and steampunk – has morphed with the zeitgeist, reflecting the social and moral concerns of our time; feminist fantasy is now popular in Europe, with books like Madeleine Miller's *Circe* (2018) retelling Greek myths from a female perspective.

RELATED TOPICS
See also
MEDIEVAL LITERATURE
page 20

GRAPHIC NOVEL
page 56

YOUNG ADULT
page 58

3-SECOND BIBLIOGRAPHY
THE WORM OUROBOROS
1922
E.R. Eddison

A GAME OF THRONES
1996
George R.R. Martin

PERDIDO STREET STATION
2000
China Miéville

THE NIGHT CIRCUS
2011
Erin Morgenstern

30-SECOND TEXT
Ella Berthoud

Fantasy comes from the Greek word meaning 'the power of the imagination to show or bring to light'.

ROMANCE

the 30-second thesis

3-SECOND PLOT
A romantic novel depicts the course of romantic love between two people with an emotionally satisfying and optimistic conclusion.

3-MINUTE THEME
Traditionally sexist and lacking in diversity, in the past, romantic novels tended to reinforce stereotypes, supporting the view that women were the passive objects of men's desire. But in recent years, romances have brought in diverse characters – men and women of different races and sexual persuasions. Today a thriving worldwide industry produces all kinds of romance, with empowered women taking their romantic destiny and sexual agency into their own hands, challenging the very precepts of the genre.

Romance is perhaps the oldest of the literary themes, with stories such as *Daphnis and Chloe* dating back to the second century CE. But the romantic novel in its modern mass-market form emerged in the 1930s when US publishing house Mills and Boon began to create escapist, romantic fiction. Though far more sophisticated than these commercial stories, the novels of Jane Austen, such as *Pride and Prejudice* (1813), are thought by many to have sowed the seeds of the genre in Britain and beyond, but writers across Europe, China and India were simultaneously writing similar tales. A romantic novel describes the love of two people who, after various setbacks, come together. Once exclusively heterosexual, the genre today more truthfully reflects society, with *The Doctor's Discretion* (2017) by E.E. Ottoman being a contemporary example of gay romantic fiction. There are many subgenres catering to readers' various romantic fantasies, including the historical romance, such as those of Georgette Heyer, paranormal romance, and the erotic, such as Kathleen Woodiwiss's *The Flame and the Flower* (1972), the latter genre having been disdainfully termed 'bodice rippers' by the literary establishment. Characterized by sexual tension, desire and idealism, romantic books gratify the reader's deepest yearnings, not just for romance but for a happily-ever-after ending.

RELATED TOPICS
See also
HISTORICAL NOVEL
page 40

LGBTQ+
page 60

3-SECOND BIBLIOGRAPHY
THE BLACK MOTH
1921
Georgette Heyer

BRING ON THE BLESSINGS
2009
Beverly Jenkins

CAPTURING THE SILKEN THIEF
2012
Jeannie Lin

HATE TO WANT YOU
2017
Alisha Rai

30-SECOND TEXT
Ella Berthoud

Love in all its guises is the subject of the romantic novel.

GRAPHIC NOVEL

the 30-second thesis

3-SECOND PLOT
A graphic novel is a book, either fiction or non-fiction, using pictures and words in an extended narrative.

3-MINUTE THEME
Manga is a style of Japanese comic book and graphic novel originating from scrolls dating back to the twelfth century, reading from right to left. In 1814, the woodcut artist Katsushika Hokusai coined the term 'manga' (translated as 'pictures running wild') which evolved from single- to multi-panel comics. Today, manga graphic novels are read worldwide and have evolved into Webtoons in South Korea – visual novels read in a continuous vertical stream online.

A graphic novel is usually made up of text and drawn images, though some, such as Shaun Tan's *The Arrival* (2006), tell a story with highly complex images but no words at all. The term was first coined in 1964 by Richard Kyle, a bookseller and writer who later published the first self-proclaimed graphic novel, George Metzger's *Beyond Time and Again* (1976). The term became widely accepted after Art Spiegelman's *Maus* was published in 1986, as this was perceived as a serious literary work in graphic novel form; and by 2001 graphic novels had their own niche in bookshops. In the West the genre evolved from the first comic novel, *The Adventures of Mr. Obadiah Oldbuck* (1837), by Rodolphe Töpffer, but the tradition of stories told with pictures has existed since ancient Greek painters depicted scenes from historical stories such as the Trojan War in horizontal narrative friezes on vases. During the nineteenth and early twentieth centuries, it was common for literary novels to be illustrated – for example, Dickens's novels were illustrated by George Cruikshank. But the decisive influence on the form of the graphic novel itself was the boom in American comics published by Marvel and DC Comics from the 1930s onwards.

RELATED TOPICS
See also
SCIENCE FICTION
page 42

FANTASY
page 52

YOUNG ADULT
page 58

3-SECOND BIBLIOGRAPHY
PERSEPOLIS
2000
Marjane Satrapi

FUN HOME
2006
Alison Bechdel

AMERICAN BORN CHINESE
2006
Gene Luen Yang

THE ARAB OF THE FUTURE
2015
Riad Sattouf

30-SECOND TEXT
Ella Berthoud

Graphic novels have increasingly found a place in mainstream bookshops over the past 20 years.

YOUNG ADULT

the 30-second thesis

3-SECOND PLOT
Young Adult novels have an adolescent protagonist who faces challenges and, mostly, emerges from the story a different, better person.

3-MINUTE THEME
The YA novel is not to be confused with the Coming-of-Age novel or Bildungsroman, which is about the transition between childhood and adulthood, and is written primarily for adults. This stage of life (becoming an adult) is particularly agonizing, illuminating and intense, and has thus inspired some of the most rewarding fiction of all time, from *Le Grand Meaulnes* (1913) by Alain-Fournier to *The Color Purple* (1982) by Alice Walker.

The literary term 'Young Adult'
was first created when S.E. Hinton wrote *The Outsiders* (1967), a novel she began when she was 15 years old. When it was published three years later, it was clear that the novel's readers were mostly her own age. Publishers realized that this group, aged 12 to 18, had their own preoccupations, and authors began to write for them, sometimes with 'problem novels' depicting extreme situations, like drug addiction, as a way to hook their interest. They placed a protagonist in their teens at the centre of the story, using changes in circumstance and character to drive the plot. Authors like Judy Blume realized that a large audience of young people was keen to read about taboo subjects, such as sex and menstruation, which she addressed unflinchingly in titles like *Forever* (1975) and *Are You There God? It's me, Margaret* (1970). Among other topics the genre explores are sexuality, first love, friendship, identity, mortality, eating disorders and suicide. The demographic has also expanded, with adults increasingly keen readers of YA fiction, in the case of cult hits such as the *Harry Potter*, *Twilight* and *Hunger Games* series, while in recent decades YA fiction has become popular in Africa, India and China.

RELATED TOPICS
See also
FANTASY
page 52

GRAPHIC NOVEL
page 56

LGBTQ+
page 60

3-SECOND BIBLIOGRAPHY
HOMECOMING
1981
Cynthia Voight

SOMEWHERE IN THE DARKNESS
1992
Walter Dean Myers

FACES IN THE WATER
2010
Ranjit Lal

THE HATE U GIVE
2017
Angie Thomas

30-SECOND TEXT
Ella Berthoud

This age group has a powerful voice in society; many authors now write stories echoing their concerns.

LGBTQ+

the 30-second thesis

Same-sex love has been

celebrated in literature since the lesbian poetry of the enigmatic Greek writer Sappho in the sixth century BCE, and later works like Petronius' *The Satyricon* (first century CE), among the earliest works of fiction to describe homosexual love. But the tolerance of the ancient world was followed by many centuries of silence during which homosexuality was taboo in most societies. In the nineteenth century, lesbian writer Wu Tsao celebrated her love of women in songs that were sung all over China, but in Europe queer literature – such as the erotic diaries of lesbian landowner Anne Lister – was suppressed. During the Age of Enlightenment, authors used allusions to Classical Greece and Rome as code for gay love, compelled by law to write allusively rather than explicitly on the subject. Then the decriminalization of homosexuality across Europe and America in the second half of the twentieth century led to an explosion of gay and lesbian writing. In many countries, LGBTQ+ literature is still banned, despite books like Jamaican writer Marlon James's *A Brief History of Seven Killings* (2014) and Iranian-American Abdi Nazemian's *The Walk-in Closet* (2014) holding out hope that one day this may change.

RELATED TOPICS
See also
ROMANCE
page 54

YOUNG ADULT
page 58

DIARY
page 68

3-SECOND BIBLIOGRAPHY
A YEAR IN ARCADIA: KYLLENION
1805
Augustus, Duke of Saxe-Gotha-Altenburg

FLOWER TALES
1916–24
Nobuko Yoshiya

THE PRICE OF SALT
1952
Patricia Highsmith

30-SECOND TEXT
Ella Berthoud

3-SECOND PLOT
LGBTQ+ literature celebrates lesbian, gay, bisexual, transgender, gender non-conforming, pansexual, questioning, intersex, asexual or queer characters.

3-MINUTE THEME
One of the fastest-growing areas of LGBTQ+ fiction is Young Adult. Teens discover their sexuality and identity at this age; where better to find role models and self-recognition than in novels and short stories? Since *I'll Get There. It Better be Worth the Trip* by John Donovan (1969) and Nancy Garden's *Annie on My Mind* (1982), YA novels have explored themes from transgender identity to bisexuality, asexuality and pansexuality with increasing mainstream success.

From Sappho to Stein to Armistead Maupin, the rainbow of sexual identities has a long history in literature.

LITERARY PROSE

LITERARY PROSE
GLOSSARY

auto-fiction Meaning fictionalized autobiography, the term was first coined by Serge Doubrovsky with reference to his novel *Fils* (1977). The form involves an autobiography of the author interwoven with fictionalized elements. This concept in writing has become increasingly popular in recent years with novel series such as Edward St Aubyn's *Melrose* books (1994–2012) and Karl Ove Knausgård's multi-volume *My Struggle* (2009–11).

autonomous A person or character having the freedom to govern themselves and their own affairs.

dissident A person who opposes, protests or challenges official policy, especially in an authoritarian state.

existential Existentialism is a system of ideas encapsulated and named by Jean Paul Sartre in the 1940s, in which he postulated that the world has no meaning, with each person entirely alone, responsible for both their actions and their fate. Sartre's novel *Nausea* (1938) is held up as a narrative manifesto of the movement.

fable A short story in verse or prose featuring animals, plants, mythical creatures or inanimate objects that are anthropomorphized in order to illustrate moral lessons.

flash fiction A very short story of 1,000 words or less.

framed tale This is a story within a story, with the framing story holding other stories within it, as in Boccaccio's *Decameron*, a fourteenth-century collection of novellas in which a group of young aristocrats fleeing the Black Death spend their time telling stories as they move through the countryside – the framing story in this case being the tale of their escape.

microfiction A subset of flash fiction – typically 300 words or less and sometimes as little as a handful of words.

philosophical novel Works of fiction in which a significant proportion of the novel is devoted to questions about the nature of existence and the purpose of life.

short-short fiction In the 1920s, flash fiction was referred to as short-short fiction and postcard fiction; the term denoted any story shorter than 1,000 words. Extremely short stories come in a bewildering array of narrowly defined categories, including the six-word story; the 280-character story designed for Twitter-length tweets, also known as 'twitterature'; the 'dribble' at 50 words, also known as the 'minisaga'; and the 'drabble' at 100 words, also known as 'microfiction'. So-called 'sudden fiction' is around 750 words, with flash fiction a little longer at 1,000 words.

travel diary A daily or regular commentary on places visited, events experienced and people encountered while travelling.

Übermensch The Superman, a superior man whose existence justifies that of the human race. The concept was defined by Friedrich Nietzsche in *Thus Spoke Zarathustra* (1883–91), who explained that the *Übermensch* would be effectively his own god, with a self-determined scope for action that would supersede existing moral codes.

SHORT STORY

the 30-second thesis

A fictional prose narrative that's longer than a couple of pages, but recognizably shorter than a novel (or, indeed, a novella), the short story is brief, concise and self-contained, usually falling between 1,000 and 15,000 words. While its precursors include both the fable and the 'framed tale', the short stand-alone story as we know it rose to prominence across Europe, the USA and beyond during the nineteenth and early twentieth centuries, in part due to the spread of print periodicals and newspapers, with Russia's Anton Chekhov, India's Rabindranath Tagore and New Zealand's Katherine Mansfield all enjoying popular and critical acclaim. This increase in popularity continued into the mid-twentieth century, thanks to the rise of US university writing programmes and the widespread circulation of literary journals like *The New Yorker* (as well as popular publications like *Playboy*). It's not all about distribution, though: in 1962, Ireland's Frank O'Connor argued that the form enjoys success because its heroes are typically not traditionally heroic, but odd, lonely, mediocre people, and that its attraction to readers lies in its particular ability to express 'an intense awareness of human loneliness' – all of which is evident in both Flannery O'Connor's Hulga ('Good Country People', 1955) and J.D. Salinger's Seymour Glass ('A Perfect Day for Bananafish', 1948).

3-SECOND PLOT
The short story is an autonomous prose narrative that clocks in, typically, at a length somewhere between 1,000 and 15,000 words.

3-MINUTE THEME
If short stories can appear somewhat condensed, given that they must convey an entire narrative in a matter of pages, they're positively extensive compared to their abbreviated cousin: flash fiction (aka microfiction or short-short fiction). Flash, at typically less than 1,000 words and an increasingly popular online form, occupies the disputed territory between prose poem and short story; among its most celebrated recent practitioners are American writer Lydia Davis and Egyptian Nobel winner, Naguib Mahfouz.

RELATED TOPICS
See also
MODERN LITERATURE
page 24

SCIENCE FICTION
page 42

HORROR
page 48

3-SECOND BIBLIOGRAPHY
A SPORTSMAN'S SKETCHES
1852
Ivan Turgenev

'THE GREAT WALL OF CHINA'
1933
Franz Kafka

KRIK? KRAK!
1996
Edwidge Danticat

RUNAWAY
2004
Alice Munro

30-SECOND TEXT
Valerie O'Riordan

Rabindranath Tagore was a master of lyrical prose, who with great wisdom captured the social panorama of Bengali life.

DIARY

the 30-second thesis

Derived from the Latin *diarium*, meaning 'daily allowance', the diary is a durational narrative telling what happened within a specific time frame; a record of events, transactions or observations. Usually private, not necessarily written to be published, the diary form allows its author to explore themselves intimately and reflect frankly upon their life and times. Among the most well-known historical examples is *The Diary of Anne Frank*. Travel diaries, such as that of nineteenth-century Swiss explorer Isabelle Eberhart, are a common form of this most quotidian of genres. Much of Charles Darwin's research into the flora and fauna of the Galapagos Islands in 1835 was reflected upon in his travel diary. The published diary, when it contains confessional or confidential material, may shock the reader, like those of literary diarist Anaïs Nin and poet Lord Byron. Writers may publish their diaries to expose concealed truths or otherwise to account for themselves, provoking or generating empathy in their readers. With the internet came a democratization of personal narrative; in the late 1990s, Open Diary and LiveJournal emerged as web-based opportunities for self-publishing diaries, soon to be overtaken by blogging and social media such as Instagram and Facebook, both popular contemporary forms of diaristic narrative.

3-SECOND PLOT
Diary is a form of literary prose that organizes memories and experiences into a durational narrative of the self, not usually intended to be published.

3-MINUTE THEME
Published diaries inspire curiosity in a readership desiring greater intimacy with public figures, celebrities and creatives. Diaries from someone's formative years can also provide fresh insight into historical players and events, such as dissident icon Che Guevara and Benjamin Franklin Bache, a figure of revolutionary and early America. Alexander Berkman's *The Bolshevik Myth* was a reflection of the Russian Revolution and its aftermath by a US anarchist revolutionary deported to Russia in 1917.

RELATED TOPICS
See also
EPISTOLARY NOVEL
page 38

AUTOBIOGRAPHY & MEMOIR
page 70

3-SECOND BIBLIOGRAPHY
THE DIARY OF SAMUEL PEPYS
1825
Samuel Pepys

THE SECRET DIARIES OF MISS ANNE LISTER (1791–1840)
1988
Anne Lister

THE DIARY OF FRIDA KAHLO
2006
Frida Kahlo

REBORN: JOURNALS AND NOTEBOOKS, 1947–63
2009
Susan Sontag

OCCUPATION DIARIES
2012
Raja Shehadeh

30-SECOND TEXT
Lauren de Sá Naylor

The diaries of both the famous and the obscure have always fascinated readers.

AUTOBIOGRAPHY & MEMOIR

the 30-second thesis

3-SECOND PLOT
Literature that gives you the honest facts (depending on how honest the author is willing to be).

3-MINUTE THEME
In addition to autobiography and autobiographical fiction, there is also auto-fiction. This seemingly paradoxical form blends autobiography and fiction, presenting a fictional first-person narrative by a narrator with the same name as the author (for example, Catherine Millet's 2001 memoir, *The Sexual Life of Catherine M.*) Notable practitioners of the form include Karl Ove Knausgård, Hitomi Kanehara and Charu Nivedita.

An autobiography is a written account of the author's own life, intended to be understood as non-fiction. The reader is provided with a series of real events, as well as insight into how these events affected the writer intellectually and emotionally. A related, but distinct, category is the memoir, which recalls a specific part of the writer's life: their childhood, for instance, or their career in politics. Politicians often write autobiographies and memoirs, either to promote their beliefs, as in Adolf Hitler's *Mein Kampf* (1925), or in an attempt to manage their legacy, as in Margaret Thatcher's *The Downing Street Years* (1993). Neither genre should be confused with autobiographical fiction, which, though made up, draws heavily on the author's lived experience and features a protagonist modelled after them; examples include Charles Dickens's *David Copperfield* (1850) and Gertrude Stein's *The Autobiography of Alice B. Toklas* (1933). Autobiography and memoir have a long history, from *Josephi Vita* (ca. 99 CE), by the first-century Jewish historian Josephus, to *Walden* (1854), Henry David Thoreau's meditation on humanity and the natural world. Today, celebrity autobiography is among the most consistently popular and widely accessible forms of literature, though many are ghostwritten by another author.

RELATED TOPIC
See also
DIARY
page 68

3-SECOND BIBLIOGRAPHY
THE BOOK OF MARGERY KEMPE
ca. 1420
Margery Kempe

NARRATIVE OF THE LIFE OF FREDERICK DOUGLASS, AN AMERICAN SLAVE
1845
Frederick Douglass

MOAB IS MY WASHPOT
1997
Stephen Fry

READING LOLITA IN TEHRAN
2003
Azar Nafisi

THE YEAR OF MAGICAL THINKING
2005
Joan Didion

30-SECOND TEXT
Lucien Young

Henry David Thoreau's memoir of living in nature has inspired imitators of its lifestyle and literary style.

15 September 1977
Born in Nigeria

1995
Studies Medicine at the
University of Nigeria

1996
Emigrates to USA to
study Communications
and Political Science
at Drexel University,
Philadelphia, then
Eastern Connecticut
State University

2003
Creative Writing Master's
Degree at John Hopkins
University

2003
Purple Hibiscus
published and receives
Commonwealth
Writer's Prize

2006
Half of a Yellow Sun
published

2008
Awarded a MacArthur
Genius Grant

2008
Master of Arts Degree
in African Studies at Yale
University

2009
TED Talk: 'The Dangers
of a Single Story'

2009
*The Thing Around Your
Neck* published

2012
TED Talk: 'We Should All
Be Feminists'

2013
Americanah published

2014
*We Should All Be
Feminists* published
in book form

2017
*Dear Ijeawele, or A
Feminist Manifesto in
Fifteen Suggestions*
published

CHIMAMANDA NGOZI ADICHIE

Chimamanda Ngozi Adichie is considered one of the most vital and original writers of her generation, and is now known as much for her hugely influential TED talks and non-fiction as for her novels. She was born one of six children in Enugu, Nigeria, to Igbo parents. She lived with her family in the house where the great Nigerian writer Chinua Achebe once resided, while her father worked as a professor of statistics at the University of Nigeria. Chimamanda studied medicine and pharmacy there, and edited a magazine for medical students called *The Compass* as a student.

She emigrated to the United States when she was 19, and studied communication and political science, eventually at Eastern Connecticut State University. During her senior year she began working on her first novel, *Purple Hibiscus*, which was published when she was only 26. She subsequently received an MA in African Studies from Yale University, and has since gone on to teach creative writing in Nigeria and the States, while continuing to write novels and short stories, and give public talks.

Her TED Talk 'The Danger of a Single Story' (2009) has been viewed by nearly 18 million people; a subsequent speech at TEDx Euston, London in 2012, 'We Should All Be Feminists', has also provoked fierce debate around the world. When this speech was sampled into a Beyoncé song, 'Flawless', her views went global. The talk became so popular that it was adapted and published as an essay by Fourth Estate in 2014. The Swedish Women's Lobby pledged to give the book to every 16-year-old in Sweden, as a springboard for debate about equality between the sexes.

Her political statements are mirrored in her novels and essays, such as in her book *Dear Ijeawele, or A Feminist Manifesto in Fifteen Suggestion*s (2014), written initially as a letter to a friend on how to raise her daughter as a feminist, outlining ideas about the roles of men and women and the preconceptions that must be smashed in order to achieve fairness between the sexes. Adichie's novels are characterized by a deep love of Nigeria, which is the bedrock of the narrative in *Purple Hibiscus* (2003) and *Half of a Yellow Sun* (2006). *Americanah* (2013) moves from Nigeria to America and reflects upon the hopes and dreams of immigrants. Adichie continues to teach, write and inspire globally.

Ella Berthoud

PHILOSOPHICAL WORKS

the 30-second thesis

Derived from the Greek

philosophia, meaning 'love of knowledge', philosophy is the source of some of the oldest and most influential world literature. In the past, the term was more generally applied to describe areas of intellectual endeavour that are now considered discrete fields of study. For instance, Isaac Newton's 1687 *Mathematical Principles of Natural Philosophy* concerns what we would now call physics. Today, philosophy is understood as an enquiry into the nature of knowledge, reality and existence. Philosophical works have played a huge role in shaping human thought, from Plato's *The Republic* (ca. 380 BCE) in the West, to Al-Ghazali's *The Revival of the Religious Sciences* (twelfth century BCE) in the Middle East. The writings of Confucius permeate Chinese culture, while those of Karl Marx provided the basis for communism. The work of philosophers Gautama Buddha and Guru Nanak became the foundations of major world religions (Buddhism and Sikhism, respectively). All narrative fiction touches on philosophical themes, but some major works are primarily about them. Friedrich Nietzsche's philosophical novel *Thus Spoke Zarathustra* (1883–91) propounds many of his theories, including the concept of the *Übermensch*.

3-SECOND PLOT
Literature that grapples with the biggest and most fundamental questions in life. Who are we? How should we behave? Is anything real?

3-MINUTE THEME
As systems of thought concerned with meaning and the nature of existence, philosophy and religion are inextricably linked. The distinction between philosophy and theology is a relatively recent one, with 'philosophy of religion' becoming a field of study in the West during the nineteenth century. It investigates religion and religious ideas from a philosophically neutral standpoint, as opposed to theology, which proceeds from religious convictions.

RELATED TOPICS
See also
EARLY LITERATURE
page 16

RELIGIOUS TEXTS
page 76

3-SECOND BIBLIOGRAPHY
SUMMA THEOLOGIAE
1265–74
St Thomas Aquinas

THE SOCIAL CONTRACT
1762
Jean-Jacques Rousseau

CRITIQUE OF PURE REASON
1781
Immanuel Kant

ON LIBERTY
1859
John Stuart Mill

THE SECOND SEX
1949
Simone de Beauvoir

30-SECOND TEXT
Lucien Young

From Plato to Proust, literature is often a vehicle for philosophical ideas.

RELIGIOUS TEXTS

the 30-second thesis

While a vast amount of literature is concerned with religion and the divine, only a few such texts have become central to a religious tradition. These sacred texts serve a variety of functions, from telling worshippers how to live a good life, to providing passages for recitation during ceremonies and rituals. They may, as in the Bible or the Qur'an, present narratives that explain the origins and destiny of humankind. Others, such as the Hindu Upanishads or Buddhist Sutras, are less narrative-based but focus more on the philosophy of that religion. Today, religious texts are more widely read and more influential than any other form of literature. The *Gutenberg Bible* was the first book printed using movable type, while the King James Version had an incalculable impact on the English language, both written and spoken. Many common idioms derive from it, including 'a fly in the ointment' and 'to put words in (one's) mouth'. Indeed, with the vast majority of writers in the West, until very recently, being steeped in Biblical language from childhood, the themes, stories and phrasing of the Bible can be found throughout the Western canon, from Milton's *Paradise Lost* (1667) to Goethe's *Faust* (1790) to Melville's *Moby Dick* (1851).

RELATED TOPICS
See also
EARLY LITERATURE
page 16

MEDIEVAL LITERATURE
page 20

PHILOSOPHICAL WORKS
page 74

3-SECOND BIBLIOGRAPHY
THE RIG VEDA
ca. 1500–1200 BCE

BODHICARYĀVATĀRA
ca. 700 CE
Shantideva

REVELATIONS OF DIVINE LOVE
late fourteenth century;
published 1670
Julian of Norwich

30-SECOND TEXT
Lucien Young

3-SECOND PLOT
Texts to live your life by, whose instruction and insight into the human condition are fundamental to their given faith.

3-MINUTE THEME
Naturally, authorship is a key issue in religious literature. Sacred texts are often held by those in the faith to have been divinely revealed or inspired. Muslims believe that the Qur'an was orally conveyed by Allah to the final prophet, Muhammad, through the archangel Gabriel (*Jibril* in Arabic). In Judaism, the Talmud asserts that the Torah was written by Moses, except for the last eight verses of Deuteronomy, which describe his death and burial.

At one time, almost every household had some form of religious literature, texts that accompanied them through life.

POETRY

POETRY
GLOSSARY

Anon An abbreviation of anonymous. Used when a poet or writer is unknown, wishes to remain unknown, or whose identity has been lost.

apostrophe A figure of speech in poetry in which the poet addresses a person or divine being they are thinking of.

bibliomancy The art of telling fortunes by opening a special book at a random spot and taking its meaning as significant.

cadence From the Latin *cadentia*, meaning 'a falling', cadence is the term that describes the rhythmical effect in a written text.

Elizabethan era The period in English history of the reign of Queen Elizabeth I (r.1558–1603).

heroic couplet A pair of rhyming iambic pentameters. They were called heroic because they appeared traditionally in long, epic poems that featured a hero. The couplets are self-contained as a grammatical unit. Here is an example from John Dryden's translation of Virgil's 'Aeneid' "Soon had their hosts in bloody battle join'd; But westward to the sea the sun declin'd."

Horatian ode A short lyric poem written in the manner of the Roman poet Horace from the first century BCE, composed in stanzas of two or four lines.

iambic pentameter A variety of metre which uses a line of verse with five metrical feet, in which each foot has one short unstressed syllable followed by a long, stressed syllable. A foot is a unit of verse that combines one stressed and at least one unstressed syllable, which is then repeated in order to establish a metre (or rhythm). The most common metrical feet in English poetry are the iamb (weak syllable followed by strong syllable e.g. gui**tar**), the trochee (strong syllable followed by weak syllable, e.g. **ham**mer), the anapest (two weak syllables followed by one strong e.g. under**stand**) and dactyl (one strong syllable followed by two weak, e.g. **mer**rily)

instapoet A poet who uses Instagram as their main platform for publishing their verse, often amassing huge numbers of followers.

kuhi Poem monuments in Japan, where haiku are carved into stone and placed around a town to give inspiration, joy and reflection to passers-by.

libertine A person who freely indulges in sensual pleasures.

lyric poem A style of poem originally written to be accompanied by a musical instrument.

metre A syllabic pattern in verse, in which stressed and unstressed syllables are deliberately weighted for effect. This provides the rhythm of the poetry.

register The register of a piece of writing refers to its level of formality.

renga A genre of Japanese collaborative poetry, written by more than one poet, and consisting of at least two *ku*, or stanzas.

Restoration The historical period in Britain from 1660 to 1689, during which the monarchy was restored, after the execution of King Charles I in 1649 and the subsequent government of Britain by Parliament under the puritan Lord Protector Oliver Cromwell.

rhetorical devices Concerned with the art of rhetoric – impressive or persuasive speaking. Rhetorical devices include repetition, hyperbole, metaphor and simile.

rhyme scheme A rhyme scheme is a method that poets use to give structure to their verse. The last word of each line will rhyme either with the next line or one further down. So ABAB means that the first and the third lines rhyme, as well as the second and fourth, while ABBA would mean that the first and fourth lines rhyme, as do the second and third.

Romanticism A movement in literature that originated in Europe in the late eighteenth century, which placed the individual at the heart of the work and emphasized imagination, our connection with nature, and the overarching importance of emotion as paramount literary qualities.

stanza A division in poetry of four or more lines which have a linking structural device such as a fixed length, metre or rhyming scheme.

Tudor Court Referring to the innermost circle of the English royal court at the time of the Tudor monarchs (1485–1063).

volta In a sonnet, the volta is the turning point of the poem where a section of the poem 'answers' the questions posed in the preceding ones – occurring in Shakespearean sonnets before the final couplet and in Petrarchan or Italian sonnets between the octave (the first eight lines) and the sestet (the last six lines).

EPIC POEM

the 30-second thesis

In the beginning, there was the epic. These ultra-long narrative poems were first composed by bards in preliterate societies, then passed down through the oral tradition. Using metre, rhyme and rhetorical devices, bards were able to memorize vast amounts of information. The oldest example recognized is the Sumerian *Epic of Gilgamesh* (ca. 2500–1400 BCE). Centuries later, the ancient Greek *Iliad* and *Odyssey*, attributed to the poet Homer, laid the foundations of Western literature. The epic would continue to flourish in written form, from ancient Rome (Virgil's *Aeneid*), to medieval Germany (the *Nibelungenlied*), and Restoration England (William Davenant's *Gondibert*). Epics generally focus on legendary figures, who change the world through heroic actions and will often come into contact or conflict with the supernatural (the Olympian Gods in the *Iliad*, *Beowulf's* Grendel). The epic dramatizes the creation of the context in which the poet and their audience exist, thus helping them to better understand it. Not all epics are so serious: Lord Byron adapted the form for *Don Juan*, a witty account of the famed libertine, which he described as an 'epic satire'. Epics are rarely composed in the modern day, though the contemporary Hindu religious leader Jagadguru Rambhadracharya has written several in Sanskrit.

3-SECOND PLOT
Great in both length and scope, the epic tells a tale of the origins of the audience for whom it was written.

3-MINUTE THEME
The origin of the epic in the oral tradition poses questions about who wrote its earliest examples. Were the *Iliad* and the *Odyssey* written by a single genius called Homer? Or are they the result of many bards telling and retelling the stories, tweaking, refining and misremembering as they went? Many scholars believe that 'Homer' is better understood as a catch-all term for a whole tradition.

RELATED TOPICS
See also
THE ORAL TRADITION
page 14

EARLY LITERATURE
page 16

SANSKRIT LITERATURE
page 18

EARLY MODERN LITERATURE
page 22

3-SECOND BIBLIOGRAPHY
METAMORPHOSES
8 CE
Ovid

AURORA LEIGH
1856
Elizabeth Barrett Browning

SRIBHARGAVARAGHAVIYAM
2002
Jagadguru Rambhadracharya

30-SECOND TEXT
Lucien Young

The epic form has been adapted by poets of many cultures, from Homer to Byron to Walcott.

FREE VERSE

the 30-second thesis

When you think of modern poetry, you're probably thinking of free verse. Traditional poetry, with its strict metrical rules and rhyming patterns, may be described as *closed-form*. Free verse, on the other hand, is *open-form*: it allows the poet to determine factors like syllable count and stanza length themselves, rather than having them imposed externally. When a writer of free verse reaches a line break, it's because they chose to put it there. Historical precursors of the form include *vers libre*, an innovation of nineteenth-century France, in which Symbolist poets like Rimbaud, Baudelaire and Laforgue relaxed the rules of metre and rhyme. American free verse seems heavily influenced by the cadencing of the Hebrew Psalms, and Walt Whitman's long, irregular lines in *Leaves of Grass* echo the rhythm and emphatic repetition of the King James Bible. In the early twentieth century, modernist poets such as Ezra Pound and Marianne Moore alighted on free verse as a means to express themselves succinctly and directly. Since then, free verse has been the dominant form of published poetry. It is the form favoured by modern 'Instapoets', such as Rupi Kaur, who have found huge audiences through sharing their verses on social media.

RELATED TOPICS
See also
MODERN LITERATURE
page 24

MODERNIST LITERATURE
page 28

POSTMODERNISM
page 148

3-SECOND BIBLIOGRAPHY
'THIS IS JUST TO SAY'
1934
William Carlos Williams

'THIS IS MY NAME'
1970
Adonis

'FLYING'
1971
Chinua Achebe

'CHINATOWN DIPTYCH'
2018
Jenny Xie

30-SECOND TEXT
Lucien Young

Walt Whitman is known as 'the father of free verse'; he revised his anthology Leaves of Grass *multiple times throughout his life.*

3-SECOND PLOT
Free verse is poetry without all the rules. The poet can use the cadences of natural speech, unconstrained by metre or rhyme scheme.

3-MINUTE THEME
Is free verse really free? William Carlos Williams argues: 'Being an art form, verse cannot be free in the sense of having no limitations or guiding principles.' It would be wrong to say that free verse doesn't follow any rules or conventions: take, for instance, its use of the poetic line. It can also be given structure through repetition of phrases, images and internal patterns of sound.

SONNET

the 30-second thesis

3-SECOND PLOT
Fourteen lines of iambic pentameter in a strict rhyme scheme. Except when it's not.

3-MINUTE THEME
A sonnet can be thought of as an argument in poetic form. The poet establishes their 'problem' in the *octet* (first eight lines) and solves it during the *sextet* (the remaining six). Frequently, there is a twist or change in tone after the eighth line. This is known as the *volta* ('turn') and marks the shift from proposition to resolution. In Shakespearean sonnets, the heroic couplet (GG) enhances a sense of closure.

The sonnet was invented in thirteenth-century Italy, most likely developed from a type of folk song (the word itself comes from the Italian *sonetto*, or '*little song*'). The greatest early sonneteer was Petrarch, whose verses were written in iambic pentameter and followed a rhyme scheme of ABBAABBA CDCDCD. As such, the Italian form is known as the Petrarchan sonnet. During the sixteenth century, the sonnet was transplanted to England by Sir Thomas Wyatt and Henry Howard. Rhymes being less common in English, the structure was adjusted to require fewer of them: the English (or Shakespearean) sonnet goes ABAB CDCD EFEF GG. This version became immensely popular at the Tudor Court, its formal constraints enabling poets to showcase their skills. The Elizabethan era saw the creation of long sonnet 'cycles', such as Sir Philip Sidney's *Astrophel and Stella* and, most famously, Shakespeare's. The English sonnet declined around the time of the Restoration, but reemerged in the Romantic era and then the twentieth century, when many examples were written worldwide. Modern poets often engage in sonnetry, playing with its formal constraints and cultural cachet. Patience Agbabi, a British poet of Nigerian descent, uses the form to explore sexuality, transnational identity and attitudes to the literary past.

RELATED TOPICS
See also
MEDIEVAL LITERATURE
page 20

EARLY MODERN LITERATURE
page 22

BALLAD
page 92

3-SECOND BIBLIOGRAPHY
'SONNET 18'
1609
William Shakespeare

'OZYMANDIAS'
1818
Percy Bysshe Shelley

'REMEMBER'
1862
Christina Rossetti

'I, BEING BORN A WOMAN AND DISTRESSED'
1923
Edna St Vincent Millay

30-SECOND TEXT
Lucien Young

Shakespeare wrote 154 sonnets, published together in 1609, as well as six that appear in his plays.

ODE

the 30-second thesis

Dignified, rarefied and sincere, odes often address their subject directly ('Hail to thee, blithe Spirit!'). This is known as *apostrophe* and is not to be confused with the punctuation mark. The ode has its roots in Classical antiquity, where it served a ceremonial purpose: to celebrate public figures, such as statesmen or athletes. The word comes from the Greek *odein* ('to chant'). Classical odes comprise three stanzas, each the same length with the same rhythm and rhyme scheme. The two main types are named Pindaric and Horatian, after their inventors, the Greek Pindar and the Roman Horace. The earliest odes in English are attributed to Edmund Spenser in the latter half of the sixteenth century. In the Romantic era, the ode was commandeered to address not the great and the good, but rather art, the natural world and human emotions. Poets such as Keats and Shelley found the form conducive to conveying their passionate fervour for these subjects, dispensing with the rigid stanza patterns of Pindar and Horace to create the irregular ode. By the twentieth century, odes had fallen almost completely out of fashion, though modern poets will sometimes employ the form's heightened register to praise public figures (ironically or otherwise).

RELATED TOPICS
See also
EARLY LITERATURE
page 16

EARLY MODERN LITERATURE
page 22

3-SECOND PLOT
A lyric poem intended to extol and elevate the person or thing addressed (for example, a loved one, solitude, a Grecian urn).

3-MINUTE THEME
Classical odes are structured in three parts: the *strophe*, the *antistrophe* and the *epode*. The *strophe* sets out the subject and sings its praises. The *antistrophe* contradicts what's come before or at least expresses another view. In the *epode*, the poet draws together the two opposing thoughts or comes down on one side. In this way, the classic ode resembles the dialectic of thesis, antithesis and synthesis.

3-SECOND BIBLIOGRAPHY
'ODE TO NEPTUNE'
1773
Phillis Wheatley

'ODE ON ADVERSITY'
1791
Mary Robinson

'DEJECTION: AN ODE'
1802
Samuel Taylor Coleridge

'THIRTY LINES ABOUT THE 'FRO'
2015
Allison Joseph

30-SECOND TEXT
Lucien Young

Romantic poets such as Shelley, Wordsworth and Keats wrote some of the best-loved odes.

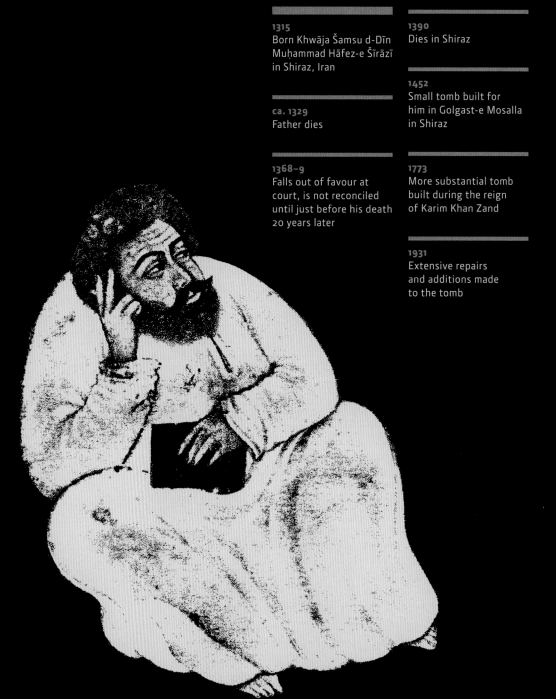

1315
Born Khwāja Šamsu d-Dīn
Muḥammad Hāfez-e Šīrāzī
in Shiraz, Iran

ca. 1329
Father dies

1368–9
Falls out of favour at
court, is not reconciled
until just before his death
20 years later

1390
Dies in Shiraz

1452
Small tomb built for
him in Golgast-e Mosalla
in Shiraz

1773
More substantial tomb
built during the reign
of Karim Khan Zand

1931
Extensive repairs
and additions made
to the tomb

HAFEZ

The name Hafez means

'memorizer' or 'safe-keeper', particularly of the teachings of the Qur'an. The poet was given this pen name because he memorized the holy book at a very early age. He is reputed to have had a phenomenal memory and learnt by heart the works of Rumi, Saadi and Nizami Ganjavi. In every Iranian home, even to this day, there are two books guaranteed pride of place: the Qur'an and *The Divan of Hafez*.

Despite being one of the most widely read and influential poets of all time, very little is known about his life. He is said to have received the gift of poetry at birth from a gypsy mystic scholar who appears very rarely to mortals. Born in Shiraz in 1315, it is believed that Hafez worked in a bakery as a young man, and while delivering bread to a rich quarter of the town, he saw Shakh-e Nabat, a woman of rare beauty to whom some of his later poems are addressed. His love for her was never requited, but it brought him to mystic states of understanding, expressed in his poetry.

Around the same time, he met Hajji Zayn al-Attar, a Persian pharmacist who became his patron, enabling him to concentrate solely on his poetry. A Shi'ite Sufi mystic, Hafez combined in his poetry the oppressed passion of the Shi'ites and the ecstatic joie de vivre of the Sufis, forming an exhilarating mix of personal and transcendental imagery. Hafez became a court poet and was widely read in his own lifetime. Around 1368 he fell out of favour at court, for reasons that are now unclear, and had to flee to Isfahan where he wrote about his beloved city of Shiraz; he was later reconciled and returned to his hometown shortly before he died.

His poetry not only explores the divine, but celebrates earthly love, desire, food and wine. Its appeal has meant that people use his writings as a resource in times of trouble, opening his books at random for guidance and inspiration. Queen Victoria herself is said to have consulted the *Fal-e-Hafez*, a collection of his writings that can be used as an oracle. His favoured poetic form was the ghazal and the collection of ghazals that form his *Divan* is most widely used for bibliomancy – the practice of telling the future from divine writings. Hafez died in Shiraz in 1390, around the age of 69. His tomb is constantly visited, sometimes by crowds in their thousands.

Ella Berthoud

BALLAD

the 30-second thesis

3-SECOND PLOT
Whether a bawdy romp,
a tale of supernatural horror
or a political broadside, the
ballad is the voice of the
people in poetic form.

3-MINUTE THEME
The question of attribution
has led to debate among
scholars of the ballad.
There are 'communalists',
who argue that traditional
ballads were the
collaborative effort of
whole communities, and
'individualists', who think
they were the work of
individual poets. The
original ballads would be
transmitted in verbal rather
than written form, which
inevitably led to them
being recomposed, either
through embellishment
or imperfect memory.

While the epic deals with the world-shaping deeds of extraordinary figures, the ballad is concerned with common folk. It often describes contemporary, local events, with street-level observers recording the traditions and travails of the world they live in. These narratives are conveyed through colloquial speech, frequently using slang and regional dialects. The ballad's down-to-earth approach stems from its origins. The word comes to us, via French, from the late Latin *ballare*, meaning 'to dance'. Wandering minstrels in Medieval Europe would set their ballads to music, accompanying dances in town and village. Given that these poets' names have been forgotten, perhaps the greatest writer of ballads is Anon. During the Romantic movement of the later eighteenth century, writers such as Robert Burns, Walter Scott and Samuel Taylor Coleridge were inspired by the folk ballad, producing their own 'literary' or 'lyrical' ballads. As Europeans colonized America and Australia, the form travelled with them, becoming the basis of the cowboy and bush ballads that flourished in the new lands. Its influence can also be seen in the nineteenth-century mixing of Anglo- and Afro-American musical styles, which gave birth to present-day popular music (and hence is why we talk about 'pop', 'R&B' and 'power' ballads).

RELATED TOPICS
See also
THE ORAL TRADITION
page 14

MEDIEVAL LITERATURE
page 20

EARLY MODERN LITERATURE
page 22

3-SECOND BIBLIOGRAPHY
'SIR PATRICK SPENS'
Anon

'MY FATHER WAS A FARMER'
1784
Robert Burns

'WALTZING MATILDA'
Banjo Paterson

'STREETS OF LAREDO'
Francis Henry Maynard

30-SECOND TEXT
Lucien Young

*Down-to-earth, musical
and meant to entertain,
ballads sang of life
on the land and those
who lived it.*

HAIKU

the 30-second thesis

Super-short Japanese poems,

which traditionally consist of seventeen *on* (roughly equivalent to English syllables). These *on* are grouped into phrases of five, then seven, then five. Most haiku focus on nature and the everyday world. By juxtaposing simple images, they aim to grant the reader intimations of the profound. Here's a translation of one by master of the form Matsuo Bashō, written in 1686: old pond / frog leaps in / water's sound. The shortest major poetic form in the world, the haiku is discrete and complete, requiring no wider context to be understood. An individual haiku has no title, as to give it one would undermine the brevity and simplicity of the work. Haiku started off as introductory verses to longer poems (*renga*). These set the tone for the whole composition, much like overtures in opera. But by the seventeenth century, standalone haiku had become increasingly common. Translations by R.H. Blyth inspired many English-language haiku in the period after the Second World War, and the form remains internationally popular to this day. In Japanese, haiku are traditionally printed in a single vertical line. In English, they usually appear in three lines, to mirror the three phrases of the Japanese form.

RELATED TOPIC
See also
SYMBOLISM
page 126

3-SECOND BIOGRAPHIES
MATSUO BASHŌ
1644–94
Elevated and popularized the haiku.

KOBAYASHI ISSA
1763–1828
Heir to Bashō who wrote over 20,000 haiku.

MASAOKA SHIKI
1867–1902
Modernized the haiku, bringing it into the twentieth century.

30-SECOND TEXT
Lucien Young

3-SECOND PLOT
This tiny poem
In seventeen syllables
Creates a whole world

3-MINUTE THEME
For centuries, haiku have been incorporated into paintings called *haiga*, in which text features alongside simple, elegant depictions of nature. Just as the haiku poet creates beauty with a minimum of syllables, so the *haiga* painter tends to use as few brushstrokes as possible. A related form is *kuhi*, whereby famous haiku are carved into natural rock, to create a sort of poetic monument. The city of Matsuyama boasts over two hundred *kuhi*.

To achieve a feeling of lightness, Bashō abandoned the old form of poetry, renga, in favour of hokku or haiku.

ふるいけや
かわずとびこむ
みずのおと

芭蕉句
三蔵言

GHAZAL

the 30-second thesis

A kind of love poem comparable to the Western sonnet or ode, the ghazal has a long and rich history. It was first developed in seventh-century Arabia, deriving from the *qasida*, an ancient, pre-Islamic poetic form. Qasidas were usually about subjects other than love, such as kings or noblemen, but featured a prelude called a *nasīb*, which would often be romantic in tenor. Eventually, poets began to write standalone *nasībs*, resulting in the ghazal. The form blossomed during the Ummayad Caliphate (661–750 CE), dividing into such sub-genres as *udharî* (concerned with courtly love), *hissî* (erotic love), *mudhakkar* (homoerotic love) and *tamhîdî* (introducing a longer poem). In the following centuries, great poets such as Rumi, Hafiz and Saadi Shirazi composed hundreds of ghazals, demonstrating the form's variety and allusive depth. Today, the ghazal is one of the most widely read poetic forms, particularly in the Middle East and South Asia. Ghazal singers, such as Jagjit Singh, have spread its influence to vast numbers of listeners. The form has also grown in popularity among Western readers during the late twentieth and early twenty-first centuries, with notable poets in English, such as Adrienne Rich, having experimented with the ghazal, often by relaxing its constraints.

RELATED TOPICS
See also
SONNET
page 86

ODE
page 88

3-SECOND BIBLIOGRAPHY
'WHERE DID THE HANDSOME BELOVED GO?'
thirteenth century
Jalal al-Din Rumi

'NO, I WASN'T MEANT TO LOVE AND BE LOVED'
nineteenth century
Mirza Asadullah Khan Ghalib

'TONIGHT'
2003
Agha Shahid Ali

'MISCEGENATION'
2007
Natasha Trethewey

30-SECOND TEXT
Lucien Young

Speaking of such things as love and longing, these poets often leave the gender of the subject ambiguous.

3-SECOND PLOT
Roughly pronounced like the English 'guzzle', this poetic form originated in Arabic and concerns matters of love and loss.

3-MINUTE THEME
The traditional ghazal obeys strict rules. It comprises a series of independent but thematically linked couplets, commonly between five and fifteen in total. The two lines of the first couplet end with the same word or phrase, which also concludes the second lines of all succeeding couplets (in a pattern known as the *radif*). The *maqtaa*, or final couplet, must include a proper name, usually that of the poet.

DRAMA

DRAMA
GLOSSARY

avant-garde A group of people who espouse startling new ideas in art, literature, music and other forms of cultural activity, including politics.

catharsis From the Greek *katharsis* meaning 'cleansing' or 'purification', this means the purification or cleansing of emotions through any art form – music, drama, literature or visual art, particularly fear and pity, resulting in a feeling of renewal, rejuvenation and restoration.

clowning Behaving in a playful or comic fashion, making fun of others, being silly, and in drama often involving improvisation as well as the humiliation of the clown.

existential Existentialism is a system of ideas encapsulated and named by Jean Paul Sartre in the 1940s, in which he postulated that the world has no meaning, with each person entirely alone, responsible for both their actions and their fate. Sartre's novel *Nausea* (1938) is held up as a narrative manifesto of the movement.

farce A kind of drama in which comedy is induced through exaggerated situations, stereotyped characters, horseplay and ridiculous circumstances born of serious ones.

flaw A literary device whereby a character has a trait that leads to his or her downfall; often this is the key protagonist in a drama, and the audience observes in horror as they see the hero or heroine causing their own downfall because of this flaw. Classic flaws include hubris, excessive ambition, cowardice or greed.

guerrilla theatre Originating from politically motivated protest theatre, guerrilla theatre aimed to highlight political issues through satire, protest and unexpected 'happenings'. Guerrilla theatre was often staged in public spaces not usually intended for the theatre. The name comes from the idea of guerrilla fighters, so named by Che Guevara during the Cuban Revolution; the intention was to destroy an unjust order, replacing an old order with a new, better one. This intention was the same with guerrilla theatre.

invisible theatre Those exposed to this form of theatre will never know that they were, as its goal is to provoke spontaneous responses while remaining unexposed as theatre. It is performed in a public space but one that is not normally used for theatre, such as a restaurant or street; bystanders will inevitably become involved, believing the theatrical events to be real life. Actors remain in character no matter what happens around them.

mime The performance of a story through movements of the body, without the use of speech.

morality play An allegorical piece of drama conveying a lesson about virtuous behaviour and good character. Popular in Europe in the fifteenth and sixteenth centuries, these plays often personified metaphysical or moral qualities, having developed from the more religious tradition of mystery plays.

paradigm An outstandingly clear or typical example, an archetype.

placard A sign held up to give extra information about characters, written in a script that is big enough for the audience to read even at the back of the theatre.

pratfalls A staged trip or fall for comedic purposes, often landing on the buttocks; a form of slapstick or physical comedy.

tableau A moment on stage when all the characters freeze into pre-ordained positions, creating a 'tableau' or still picture that will cause the audience to notice and ponder its meaning; this effect also draws attention to the fact that the actors are indeed acting, in doing so undermining any sense of realism.

vaudeville Light musical theatre interspersed with songs; thought to be a corruption of Vaux-de-Vire, satirical songs in couplets sung to popular tunes in the fifteenth century in the Val-de-Vire in Normandy, France.

Yoruba The name given to the Yoruba language, religion and people, whose homeland is in present-day south-western Nigeria and the neighbouring parts of Benin and Togo, collectively known as Yorubaland.

TRAGEDY

the 30-second thesis

RELATED TOPIC
See also
THEATRE OF THE ABSURD
page 110

3-SECOND BIBLIOGRAPHY
OEDIPUS REX
429 BCE
Sophocles

THE TRAGEDY OF MARIAM
1613
Elizabeth Cary

WOYZECK
1913
Georg Büchner

PHAEDRA'S LOVE
1996
Sarah Kane

THE FERRYMAN
2017
Jez Butterworth

30-SECOND TEXT
Charlotte Raby

3-SECOND PLOT
Tragedy is the enactment of the existential question: do we have volition or are we just pawns moved by the hand of fate?

3-MINUTE THEME
Tragedy is not universal, as some claim the current rise of tragedy may reflect the perceived importance of the individual in certain cultures, with the audience suffering alongside the protagonist as they struggle against an impossible situation. In *Death and the King's Horseman* (1975), Soyinka uses the chasm of understanding between two cultures to reflect on free will and the meaning of death in a ritual context in the life of a traditional Yoruba community.

The Greeks (fifth century BCE) used tragedy to explore why humans suffer. The plays of Aeschylus, Sophocles and Euripides ask whether this suffering was due to human flaws or the malice of the gods. These stories partnered a royal protagonist or hero with a fatal flaw that led them to make terrible mistakes, creating a potent plot in which they realize their errors but cannot resist the impending catastrophe made inevitable by the fates, and the irresistible trajectory of their flawed existence. Aristotle described the pleasure of witnessing tragedy as a catharsis leading to purification, restoring the audience's spirits. After the Greeks, tragedy disappeared for nearly 2,000 years until 1561, when the first English tragedy, *Gorboduc* by Thomas Norton and Thomas Sackville, was performed for Queen Elizabeth I. The plays of Shakespeare and Marlowe that followed created the template for modern tragedy, where serious plays explore how humans create their own misery, with the dynamics of power, sex, gender and culture taking the place of the fates. Plays by Federico García Lorca, Henrik Ibsen and August Strindberg focus on sexual power, ending in blood and death, while Wole Soyinka uses colonial rather than divine power in a tragedy caused by two forces at fatal odds.

In ancient Greece there were three Fates: Clotho spun the thread of human fate; Lachesis dispensed it; and Atropos cut it.

COMEDY

the 30-second thesis

3-SECOND PLOT
While exploiting the comic potential of others' misfortunes or exposing the flaws of those in power, comedy also helps an audience to laugh at itself.

3-MINUTE THEME
The philosopher Thomas Hobbes called laughter the 'sudden glory', which arises from recognizing our own fallibility or seeing our goodness contrasted with another's foolishness. In ancient Sanskrit drama (from around 200 BCE) humour (hāsyam) is one of the nine principal emotions (rasas) that combine to transport audiences to a parallel reality. In Sanskrit plays, humour bridges the chasm created by opposition, lifting us beyond simply laughing at others' misfortunes into laughing at the absurdity of life.

Be it actors wearing massive red leather phalluses, identical twins causing confusion, gender mix-ups, pratfalls, the intricate timing of a bedroom farce or the joy at seeing a recognizable figure being satirized, comedy is integral to theatre. In ancient Greece, comedy was one of the three principal dramatic forms. Greek comedy included satire, sexual innuendo and farce, as found in the surviving plays of Aristophanes. The philosopher Aristotle believed that comedy was positive for society, inducing the ideal state of happiness; to that end, for both ancient Greeks and Romans comedy was a stage-play with a happy ending, a paradigm that also applies to the ten comedies of Shakespeare, which all 'end well', often with a marriage. Perhaps because it reflects society and performs a vital function in holding power to account, of all the comedic forms it is satire which runs like a golden thread through the ages from the Greeks to present-day theatre. The Romans divided satire into two types: Juvenalian which lashes out at its victims without mercy, contemporary examples of which include *Home, I'm Darling* (2018) by Laura Wade and David Adjmi's *3C* (2012); and Horatian, which is kinder, with George C. Wolfe's *The Colored Museum* (1986) a notable modern example.

RELATED TOPICS
See also
SANSKRIT LITERATURE
page 18

SATIRE
page 144

3-SECOND BIBLIOGRAPHY
MARRIAGE
1842
Nikolay Gogol

THE IMPORTANCE OF BEING EARNEST
1895
Oscar Wilde

THE BOOK OF LIZ
2002
Amy and David Sedaris

BURQAVAGANZA
2008
Shahid Nadeem

30-SECOND TEXT
Charlotte Raby

Visual japes are integral to theatrical comedy, the inventiveness of both director and actors are as important as the script.

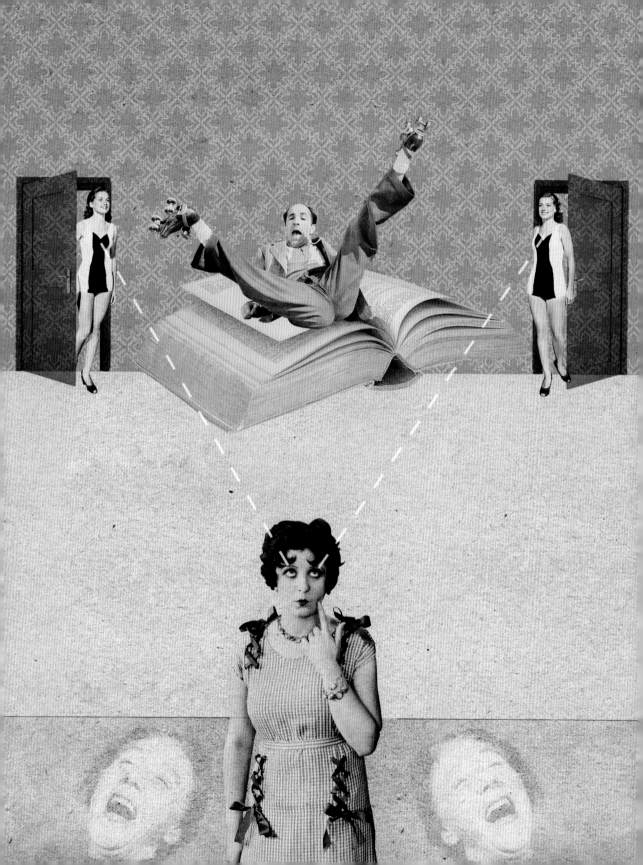

ca. 450 BCE
Born in Cydathenae
in Athens

423 BCE
The Clouds first
performed

422 BCE
The Wasps first
performed – it wins
second place at the
Lenaia competition.

421 BCE
Peace first performed
(promising an end to the
Peloponnesian War)

414 BCE
The Birds first performed

ca. 411 BCE
Thesmophoriazusae first
performed

411 BCE
Lysistrata first performed

408 BCE
Plutus first performed

405 BCE
Frogs first performed
and wins first place in
Lenaia, a festival of
Dionysus in Athens

388 BCE
Plutus revised
and performed
again in Athens

ca. 386 BCE
Dies

ARISTOPHANES

Born ca. 450 BCE in Athens, Aristophanes spent his boyhood in the cultural centre of Greece. He was born into a wealthy family and was well read, with a good knowledge of Homer and the Greek philosophers. His career as a dramatist began when he was only a teenager, with a play called *The Banqueters* (427 BCE; now lost), a satire of contemporary morality. He won second prize in the annual Athens dramatic competition for this play, and the next year he won first prize for *The Babylonians*, though this play (426 BCE; also lost) caused controversy at the time, and was called a slander against the Athenian citizens by Cleon, a prominent general in the army. In return, Aristophanes lampooned Cleon in his next play, *The Knights* (424 BCE).

Few people of note at the time escaped his satire, including his fellow dramatists: Sophocles was ridiculed in *The Clouds* (423 BCE), and Euripides in *The Frogs* (405 BCE). Throughout his life, Aristophanes was also much concerned with his country's bellicose activities. The plot in *The Birds* (414 BCE) was a fantastical conceit in which the birds built a city suspended between heaven and earth, where they could have mastery over humans. It was seen as a satire on the Athenians' imperialistic dreams. Banging a similar drum with its themes of pacifism and sexual rebellion, *Lysistrata* is now Aristophanes' most regularly performed play, written as an anti-war polemic in which one woman decides to end the Peloponnesian War by persuading all the womenfolk in Athens to withhold sex from their husbands until they stop fighting. It has been re-worked countless times and in 2015 was made into a film, *Chiraq*, by Spike Lee, set in the ganglands of Chicago.

He is thought to have written 40 plays in total, of which 11 are extant. Full of puns, witticisms and topical allusions, firmly rooted in their time and yet eternally appealing, they are the only surviving examples of Old Comedy, which used burlesque, satire and an abundance of scatological and sexual references. However, in 404 BCE, Athens was defeated by the Spartans, and comedy became less openly satirical and outrageous. Aristophanes' particular brand of comedy fell out of favour, and Aristophanes had to hold his tongue. He died in his beloved Athens ca. 386 BCE.

Ella Berthoud

MELODRAMA

the 30-second thesis

Melodrama is often a pejorative term describing morality tales of swooning virgins and lascivious lotharios. Yet in its time it was critical in bringing theatre to the newly urbanized middle classes of the eighteenth and nineteenth centuries. It emerged as a reaction to dramatic social political change, namely, the American Revolutionary War and the French Revolution. Plays such as Edward Fitzball's *John Bradford, or, The murder at the road-side inn* (1835) and Douglas Jerrold's *Black-eyed Susan* (1829) drew vast audiences in theatres that seated up to 4,000 people. The scale of these productions required a grand acting style and the creation of fantastic stage effects for melodramatic moments such as lake rescues or a train hurtling towards a heroine tied to the track – ideas that became staples of early cinema. Melodrama may have originated in medieval morality plays, placing ordinary people in extreme dilemmas, but the modernized eighteenth-century melodrama used sexual assault by aristocrats upon young middle-class women as a metaphor for class conflict. The melodramatic tropes and stereotypes were: the evil temptress, the fallen woman, the single mother, orphans and a man struggling with the changing world around him. Although there are few melodramas on stage now it persists today in television soap operas around the world.

3-SECOND PLOT
Melodrama was synonymous with huge audiences, vast theatres, incredibly inventive sets and high moral drama about good and evil – but always with a happy ending.

3-MINUTE THEME
Melodrama examined unsettling aspects of class conflict through the lens of the new morality. It had transnational appeal. British melodramas travelled to America, Australia and throughout Europe. Plays from America such as Harriet Beecher Stowe's *Uncle Tom's Cabin* (1852) were very successful in London theatres. European melodramas such as Pixérécourt's *La Femme à deux maris* (1802), often accompanied by an orchestra, were also popular in the London theatres.

RELATED TOPIC
See also
ROMANCE
page 54

3-SECOND BIBLIOGRAPHY
A TALE OF MYSTERY
1802
Thomas Holcroft

THE FACTORY LAD
1832
John Walker

A WOMAN OF NO IMPORTANCE
1893
Oscar Wilde

BREAKER MORANT: A PLAY IN TWO ACTS
1978
Kenneth G. Ross

30-SECOND TEXT
Charlotte Raby

The extreme display of gesture and emotion in melodrama was developed to entertain audiences in vast auditoria.

THEATRE OF
THE ABSURD

the 30-second thesis

It should be no surprise that post-Second World War plays were full of anxiety, uncertainty and existential dismay, yet much of the most avant-garde theatre was funny and irreverent as well as provocative and unsettling. In 1961, in a book of the same name the producer and dramatist Martin Esslin described a group of playwrights of the period whose work exhibited these traits as constituting 'the theatre of the absurd'. Absurdism, he insisted, had 'renounced arguing *about* the absurdity of the human condition; it merely *presents* it in being…' Many of these dramatists lived in exile in Paris, and their bizarre, vaudevillesque plays drew on a theatrical heritage including mime, clowning and nonsense verse. They wrote about man's estrangement from society (Eugène Ionesco's *Rhinoceros*, 1959), life's futility (Samuel Beckett's *Endgame*, 1957) and the alienation and the violence of language (Harold Pinter's *Mountain Language*, 1988). Plays such as Beckett's *Waiting for Godot* (1953) debuted in the tiny theatres of the Latin Quarter in Paris and were abhorred by the critics. But *Godot* was soon recognized as a masterpiece on the futility of the human condition. It has since been translated into many languages and performed across the globe.

3-SECOND PLOT

Absurdist theatre embraces absurdity in all its forms – philosophical, dramaturgical, existential and emotional – in a context where nothing happens beyond the perplexing mundanity of life.

3-MINUTE THEME

After a world war in which humanity had shown both its best and worst side, absurdist theatre exposed the central contradictions of the human condition. These intriguingly mirror one of the Four Noble Truths of Buddhism, called *Dukkha*: that we crave and cling to impermanent things and for that reason are incapable of achieving happiness. The characters in absurdist plays are ceaselessly searching for truth, hope and meaning, yet remain trapped in cycles of ignorance.

RELATED TOPICS

See also
MODERNIST LITERATURE
page 28

SHORT STORY
page 66

PHILISOPHICAL WORKS
page 74

3-SECOND BIBLIOGRAPHY
THE SANDBOX
1959
Edward Albee

TANGO
1965
Sławomir Mrożek

THE BUS STOP
1981
Gao Xingjian

FUDDY MEERS
1999
David Lindsay-Abaire

30-SECOND TEXT
Charlotte Raby

The epidemic of rhinoceroses in Ionesco's Rhinoceros (1959) was an allegory for the rise of Nazism and Fascism in Europe.

PASSION PLAY

the 30-second thesis

3-SECOND PLOT
Passion plays are religious plays acting out the pain and ecstasy of a religious figure facing death and suffering in the cause of human redemption.

3-MINUTE THEME
The *Oberammergau*, which takes place in the village of that name in the Bavarian Alps, was written in the fifteenth and sixteenth centuries. It is famous for having been performed without fail every tenth year since 1634, fulfilling a covenant with God made by the town in return for being spared the bubonic plague. The 2,000 actors in the play are all town residents, with the eight-hour performance today drawing audiences of 500,000.

Passion plays are plays enacting

the passion and transfiguration of religious figures. The universal themes of pain, injustice and death, leading to forgiveness, redemption and hope are central to any Passion play. Every Easter across the globe, Christian Passion plays re-enact the final days of Jesus Christ. Originating from the Christian liturgy, these plays are not without controversy: portrayals of Jews as villains have led to anti-Semitic violence throughout history, even to the present day. The *Ta'ziyeh* is an Islamic Passion play; a religious epic of Iranian origin, commemorating the martyrdom of the third Imam of the Shi'ite Muslims, Ali Hussein, and his family in the desert of Kerbala. In *Ta'ziyeh*, actors read or sing from their scripts, rather than act, preserving the spiritual truth of the text. Originally performed outdoors, *Ta'ziyeh* are now staged in bespoke structures called *Takiyeh* or *Hussainiyeh*. The Hindu epic, the *Ramlila of Ramnagar*, is another form of passion play, telling the story of Rama's defeat of evil. The play, performed annually in Varanasi, India for the past 200 years, lasts 31 days, attracting audiences of up to a million. All these plays channel the audience's sorrows and desires as an expression of their faith; actors and audience experience an emotional reaction similar to catharsis after watching tragedy.

RELATED TOPICS
See also
RELIGIOUS TEXTS
page 76

TRAGEDY
page 102

30-SECOND TEXT
Charlotte Raby

The epic passion play performed once every decade in Oberammergau, Germany draws believers and non-believers alike.

POLITICAL PLAY
the 30-second thesis

Since the mid-twentieth century, in seeking to challenge the power of existing elites, political theatre in many forms has sought to be a theatre of, by and for the people. German playwright Bertolt Brecht believed the climactic catharsis of most plays left the audience complacent, which led him to develop the idea of 'epic theatre'. These plays were staged in such a way that the audience could not mistake the play for reality: harsh bright lights, tableaux, explanatory placards and spoken stage directions deliberately estranged the audience from the play, leaving them space to be self-reflective. Brecht saw his plays not as 'his' but as belonging to the 'Brechtian collective' of writers, composers, directors and actors with whom he worked. His methods and ideas have influenced political playwrights throughout the world. He inspired Brazilian theatre practitioner Augusto Boal's 'Theatre of the Oppressed', including techniques such as 'forum theatre', where spectators shape the action by calling out suggestions for the actors to improvise; and 'invisible theatre', where performances are staged in unusual places such as carparks or the street. These plays made the audience integral to the play, bringing the political into everyday places and to everyone, including those who would never normally go to the theatre.

3-SECOND PLOT
In many theatrical forms the audience is impotent, but political theatre is designed to involve the audience and provoke them into action resulting in change.

3-MINUTE THEME
Both guerrilla theatre, which originated in San Francisco in 1965, and The Living Theatre – created by Judith Malina and Julian Beck in 1947 – used public places for performances pushing overt political messages against the Vietnam War, for example, or capitalism. In a similar way to Boal, they hoped to shock unsuspecting audiences into action, preparing them mentally and emotionally for the revolution needed to overthrow the existing political order.

RELATED TOPIC
See also
POSTMODERNISM
page 148

3-SECOND BIBLIOGRAPHY
THE ROMANS IN BRITAIN
1980
Howard Brenton

FEN
1983
Caryl Churchill

DEATH AND THE MAIDEN
1990
Ariel Dorfman

AFTER INDEPENDENCE
2016
May Sumbwanyambe

AN EVENING AT THE OPERA
2016
Floy Quintos

THE JUNGLE
2017
Joe Murphy & Joe Robertson

30-SECOND TEXT
Charlotte Raby

Brecht highlighted the artifice of theatre so that audiences would not be complacent.

LITERARY DEVICES

LITERARY DEVICES
GLOSSARY

anachrony A discrepancy between the true order of events and the order in which they are represented in the plot of a narrative; refers to flashbacks and flashforwards, which are often used in fragmented narratives.

analepsis A device in narrative in which a past event is narrated at a later point than its chronological order; otherwise known as a flashback.

anthropomorphism The attribution of human characteristics to an object, animal or god; a device favoured by writers of fables and allegories.

dramatic irony The use of language in a way that would normally signify the opposite of what one intends to be understood; a technique in drama where the character is unaware of something that the audience fully understands.

gijinka or **gijinhō** The humanization of any animal-like character in Japanese art, graphic novels, comics and video art, used also to denote entities such as internet browsers. It is anthropomorphism by another name.

humanism A philosophical and ethical stance that rejects superstition and unsubstantiated faith in favour of critical thinking and evidence.

Panchatantra A collection of interrelated animal fables held within a frame story written around 200 BCE, based on an older oral tradition and written in Sanskrit verse and prose.

parable A simple story intended to illustrate a moral message, particularly in the New Testament as told by Jesus Christ, but also common in most world religions and folklore tales such as the near ubiquitous 'The Boy Who Cried Wolf'. This form of story uses simile and metaphor to demonstrate a moral lesson.

prolepsis A figure of speech in which a future act is represented as having already occurred; also known as a flashforward.

rhetoric Language intended to have a persuasive or powerful effect, often without meaningful content.

sarcasm The use of language to mock or undermine, frequently by saying the exact opposite of what is meant in order to hurt or emotionally attack.

Shintoism Meaning 'the way of the gods', Shinto is the major religion in Japan alongside Buddhism. It has no founder or dogma but its beliefs include the worship of invisible spiritual forces within nature or of ancestors and guardians. It was the state religion of Japan until 1945.

ultraists Ultraism was a literary movement born in Spain in 1919, launched by the poet Guillermo de Torre. Ultraists rejected the previous movement of 'Modernismo', which was ornate and sought beauty in the structure of language, and opted instead for free verse and evocative imagery. The short-lived journal *Ultra* was the core of the Ultraism movement and when it ceased printing in 1922 the movement declined, though Jorge Luis Borges took the ideas of Ultraism with him to South America.

verbal irony A direct contradiction between what is meant and what is said, when words express something contrary to the truth, or an actor on stage says the opposite of what they really feel or mean; as opposed to dramatic irony, in which the audience sees something that the actor is seemingly unaware of.

IRONY

the 30-second thesis

RELATED TOPICS
See also
TRAGEDY
page 102

COMEDY
page 104

SATIRE
page 144

3-SECOND BIBLIOGRAPHY
'THE GIFT OF THE MAGI'
1905
O. Henry

WHAT DO YOU WANT FROM ME?
1991
Doris Dörrie

THE HOUSE GUN
1998
Nadine Gordimer

WAITING FOR THE WILD BEASTS TO VOTE
1998
Ahmadou Kourouma

3-SECOND PLOT
Verbal irony describes a contradiction between what's said and what's meant; dramatic irony reveals incongruities between what's expected to happen and what actually is happening.

3-MINUTE THEME
Britain's First World War poets made use of verbal irony to highlight the discrepancy between what they saw as the glorification of war in patriotic rhetoric, and the reality of the trenches. Wilfred Owen's 'Dulce et Decorum Est' (1917) describes the horror of a gas attack ('Obscene as cancer, bitter as the cud / Of vile, incurable sores') and contrasts this with Roman poet Horace's then-popular dictum: 'it is sweet and good to die for your country'.

A linguistic and literary term used

to describe a discrepancy between what *seems* to be going on and what's *actually* going on, irony is often misunderstood as referring to a simple contrast between expectations and reality, when it's actually more to do with the difference between the *surface* meaning of something and its *underlying* meaning. In literature, it's often used for comedic, dramatic or tragic ends, upending the character's (or the reader's, or audience's) prior assumptions: Henry VIII's drawn-out pursuit of Anne Boleyn in Hilary Mantel's *Wolf Hall* (2009) relies on dramatic irony to the extent that the readers know what neither Henry, Anne nor Henry's fixer, Thomas Cromwell, do: that Anne is never going to bear Henry his longed-for male heir. This awareness lends the plot an air of tragedy and menace that contrasts sharply with the characters' self-satisfaction. In *Pygmalion* (1913), George Bernard Shaw's Professor Higgins puts on a grand display of verbal irony by swearing angrily that he 'never swears'. Sarcasm is a sub-set of verbal irony: it's always mean-spirited. Irony was used extensively in Ancient Greek writings, and it has long been a key device in literary satire, used to highlight societal or political contradictions and shortcomings.

30-SECOND TEXT
Valerie O'Riordan

In Shakespeare's **Othello**, *Desdemona's supposed infidelity is represented by her handkerchief.*

ALLEGORY

the 30-second thesis

An allegory is a story with both a literal and a figurative meaning. The origins of allegory can be traced to Homer and his use of the gods Phobos and Deimos in the *Iliad* (eighth century BCE), where Phobos personifies fear and panic, and Deimos dread and terror. Allegory is also used extensively in The Bible – for example, the Parables of Jesus – and was a vital element in medieval literature, including works such as Dante's *Divine Comedy* (1320). Characters and events in allegorical literature represent concepts or qualities with a moral, religious or political meaning. Ideas that are often complex to understand or critical in a way that would be unacceptable or even dangerous to communicate directly, such as when writers use allegory to disapprove of a political regime, are often more effectively communicated through allegory. *The Master and Margarita* (1967) by Mikhail Bulgakov is an allegorical novel, a commentary on Stalin's regime set in a chaotic version of Moscow where people often disappear without explanation. There is a secret police force, groups are known by acronyms, and lavish lifestyles are indulged in a society meant to be classless. Allegory is used across genres and in contemporary literature is often to be found in science fiction.

3-SECOND PLOT
An allegory is a story which uses characters and events to represent something else, often with a political, religious or moral meaning.

3-MINUTE THEME
An allegory is an extended metaphor. A metaphor is when something is compared directly to something else in order to provide clarity of meaning or to highlight similarities between two things. It is often used in speeches and occurs in all forms of literature. In Paulo Coehlo's *The Alchemist* (1988) the journey the protagonist, Santiago, undertakes is a metaphor for life. It compares an actual journey to the Egyptian pyramids to the search for destiny and meaning.

RELATED TOPICS
See also
MEDIEVAL LITERATURE
page 20

SCIENCE FICTION
page 42

RELIGIOUS TEXTS
page 76

3-SECOND BIBLIOGRAPHY
THE PILGRIM'S PROGRESS
1678
John Bunyan

HINDS' FEET ON HIGH PLACES
1955
Hannah Hunnard

A WRINKLE IN TIME
1962
Madeleine L'Engle

LIFE OF PI
2001
Yann Martel

30-SECOND TEXT
Naomi Frisby

The giant cat in **The Master and Margarita** *is an allegory for the unpredictable evils of Stalinist Moscow.*

24 August 1899
Born in Buenos Aires

1914
Travels with his family to Europe; becomes stranded in Switzerland

1921
Returns to Argentina

1937
Given job at the municipal library in Buenos Aires

1938
Suffers severe head wound and nearly dies

1941
The Garden of Forking Paths (short stories) published

1944
Fictions (short stories) published

1946
Fired from job at library, becomes lecturer in English and American Literature

1949
The Aleph and Other Stories published

1953
Becomes completely blind

1955
Appointed director of National Public Library

1957
The Book of Imaginary Beings published

1961
Receives Prix Formentor and comes to international attention

1962
Labyrinths (short stories) published

1971
Wins Jerusalem Prize

1975
The Book of Sand (short stories) published

14 June 1986
Dies in Geneva

JORGE LUIS BORGES

Jorge Luis Borges has had a unique and powerful influence on world literature. He wrote across genres: philosophical essays, poems, short stories and translations, even literary forgeries. He is known for his fantastical literary journeys and is credited with being the inventor of Magic Realism.

Born in Argentina in 1899, Jorge Luis Borges grew up speaking Spanish and English equally; his father had a large library of books that Borges later described as the key to his life. With hereditary poor eyesight and a delicate constitution, Borges spent his youth reading and extemporizing on ideas with his family. When he was 15, the family travelled to Switzerland for a holiday, but were caught up in the First World War and stayed in Europe for the next seven years. In Madrid, the young Borges was drawn to a new literary group called the 'ultraists', who used free verse and embraced new technology, rejecting sentimentalism. It was through them that he realized he did not need to adhere to any one tradition or form in literature, but could call himself a free thinker.

Returning to Argentina in 1921, Borges was strongly influenced by his father's friend, the poet Macedonio Fernández, whose complex philosophical conceits and brilliant conversation challenged Borges and drew out his own ideas. The young poet produced an ultraist magazine called *Prisma*, then in 1923 published his first book of poems. He was employed in the public library of Buenos Aires, but eventually left the job to become a lecturer in English and American Literature at the university.

His first collection of short stories, *The Garden of Forking Paths*, was published in 1941. His stories are famous for the use of intertextual references, self-reflection, notions of hyperreality and various playful devices. He posed the conundrum: does the writer write the story, or does the story write him? For many years he contributed to literary magazines and wrote film reviews – until he lost his sight, aged 55. It was not until 1961 that his work came to international attention, by which time the loss of his sight meant that he had to dictate his work to his mother, with whom he lived until she died aged 99. Increasingly he turned to poetry, being still able to work on a poem in his head. He died of liver cancer aged 86, having married his personal assistant, Maria Kodama, not long before.

Ella Berthoud

SYMBOLISM

the 30-second thesis

Authors use symbols to signify

ideas or qualities, investing abstract meanings in all kinds of objects, colours, animals or plants for the purposes of metaphor and thematic or character development. For example, a ring can symbolize fidelity and eternity, a white flower innocence. Across all cultures and millennia, authors reflecting the world they describe have used symbols to convey the underlying meanings of their stories. Virgil's fire in *The Aeneid* (ca. 29–19 BCE) symbolizes unbridled energy for either good or ill – the fire that might destroy Troy, the fire that burns in Dido's veins; the Wife of Bath's red stockings in Chaucer's *Canterbury Tales* (1392) denote her lust; the love potion in Shakespeare's *A Midsummer Night's Dream* (ca. 1595) is a symbol of the fickleness and unpredictability of love. Writers deliberately repeat symbols so as to emphasize and augment the metaphorical allusion they are making, as in *Journey to the West* by Wu Ch'eng En (ca. 1550), where stone is used repeatedly as a symbol for fearlessness and attachment to earthly sentiments. In some cases the whole of a work of literature can be a symbol, as in Chimamanda Ngozie Adichie's *Purple Hibiscus* (2003), in which the titular flower is a symbol for freedom from oppression.

3-SECOND PLOT
Authors use symbols in the form of physical objects or sensory phenomena to represent ideas or qualities integral to the meaning of the story.

3-MINUTE THEME
Symbolism has often been employed by writers living in oppressive regimes to express dissident sentiments through metaphor, to avoid openly criticizing a dictatorial government. For example, in Chinese writer Lu Xun's short story *Some Rabbits and a Cat* (1922), the baby rabbits represent the downtrodden common people, the cat is the oppressive political system in China at the time and the mother of the bunnies is Mother China, portrayed as a failing matriarch.

RELATED TOPICS
See also
SONNET
page 86

ALLEGORY
page 122

3-SECOND BIBLIOGRAPHY
WUTHERING HEIGHTS
1847
Emily Brontë

MOBY DICK
1851
Herman Melville

ANNA KARENINA
1877
Leo Tolstoy

THE BEAUTIFUL ONES ARE NOT YET BORN
1968
Aye Kwei Armah

LOVE IN THE TIME OF CHOLERA
1985
Gabriel García Márquez

30-SECOND TEXT
Ella Berthoud

Flowers are universal symbols of purity, innocence, love and desire.

ANTHROPOMORPHISM

the 30-second thesis

The literary device whereby a
writer ascribes human characteristics (physical
and psychological) and/or behaviours to non-
humans – typically gods and animals, but
sometimes natural phenomena or objects –
anthropomorphism comprises the Greek
words ánthrōpos ('human') and morphē ('form').
Folk and childrens' literatures are widely
populated with anthropomorphized creatures:
from the ancient Sanskrit *Panchatantra* to
Harry Potter's Dobby, the device is often
invoked in a spirit of education or easy-to-digest
morality tales for younger readers. In the UK,
the Renaissance turn to humanism caused the
temporary collapse of literary anthropomorphism,
but it was revived by Anna Sewell's *Black Beauty*
(1877), a book that drew critical attention to
animal welfare. While many writers have used
the device to educate and/or entertain, others
have used it as a way of cloaking – or rendering
more palatable – political messages via allegory
or satire. The Asante tales of Anansi the spider,
which originated in seventeenth-century Ghana,
spreading subsequently to Côte d'Ivoire, Sierra
Leone and beyond, used a series of comic animal
adventures to model a spirit of community and
resistance for enslaved peoples. Contemporary
graphic fiction, too, has a strong anthropomorphic
component, with Japan's webcomic *Hetalia*
giving human form to nation-states.

3-SECOND PLOT
Anthropomorphism is
a long-standing literary
technique that aims to
make its non-human object
credibly and consistently
behave exactly as if it
were human.

3-MINUTE THEME
While Judaism and Islam
forbid representation
of their deities,
anthropomorphism featured
heavily in many ancient
mythologies and religions,
with the Mesopotamians,
Canaanites/Ugaritics,
ancient Egyptians and
Hittites all embodying
their gods in human, or
human-like, form. Japanese
Shintoism has a similarly
strong animistic tradition,
reflected in the continuing
prevalence of *gijinka* or
gijinhō in contemporary
Japanese literature. Haruki
Murakami's *Kafka on the
Shore* (2002) highlighted
this tradition for
international audiences.

RELATED TOPICS
See also
ALLEGORY
page 122

PERSONIFICATION
page 130

SATIRE
page 144

3-SECOND BIBLIOGRAPHY
AESOP'S FABLES
collected 620–564 BCE
Aesop

JUST SO STORIES
1902
Rudyard Kipling

ANIMAL FARM
1945
George Orwell

THREE BAGS FULL
2007
Leonie Swann

30-SECOND TEXT
Valerie O'Riordan

*Bestowing animals and
objects with human
qualities is an innate
human habit.*

PERSONIFICATION

the 30-second thesis

Personification helps the reader

to visualize an object or idea by applying human qualities and traits to it, such as emotions, desires, sensations, gestures and speech. Writers use personification to create vivid imagery, drawing the reader into a deeper relationship with the text. Assuming a shared understanding of what it is to be human, the poet imparts human qualities to non-human phenomena – ideas or objects – lending them an immediacy that dramatizes areas of experience the reader might otherwise view indifferently. The image often contains multiple layers, particularly in poetry, leaving the reader to contemplate the different meanings. In the opening line of *The Waste Land*, T.S. Eliot describes April as 'the cruellest month'. A month cannot be cruel, however, so we understand him to mean that it is cold; that glimpses of the sun encourage us to anticipate the spring, which is yet to arrive. We often use personification as part of our everyday language. For example, when we describe nature as Mother Nature, we are implying that the natural world is feminine and, specifically, that it has the same caring and nurturing qualities we ascribe to mothers.

3-SECOND PLOT
Personification is the giving of human qualities to non-human things. It helps the reader to imagine an idea or object more vividly.

3-MINUTE THEME
Personification and anthropomorphism can be easily confused. Anthropomorphism refers solely to animals being made to act, and sometimes look, like humans, while personification is the technique of giving ideas and objects human characteristics to make them appear more vivid. George Orwell used anthropomorphism in *Animal Farm* to enable him to disguise the Russian leaders he was criticizing.

RELATED TOPICS
See also
SONNET
page 86

ODE
page 88

ANTHROPOMORPHISM
page 128

3-SECOND BIBLIOGRAPHY
'I WANDERED LONELY AS A CLOUD'
1804
William Wordsworth

'THE MIRROR'
1961
Sylvia Plath

'FOR FOREST'
1988
Grace Nichols

'RAIN AT THREE'
2018
Tishani Doshi

30-SECOND TEXT
Naomi Frisby

By giving life to objects or ideas in literature, we gain a new perspective on our world.

FORESHADOW & FLASHBACK

the 30-second thesis

3-SECOND PLOT
Flashbacks and
foreshadowing allow the
writer to play with narrative
time; they complicate the
chronological sequencing
of a story to create a more
dynamic plot.

3-MINUTE THEME
While analepsis is
frequently and seamlessly
incorporated into texts as a
function of the characters'
memories, prolepsis is a
more evident display of
authorial control: Ian
McEwan's *Atonement*
(2001), for instance, is
littered with glimpses of
the narrator's future that
highlight her present
innocence, and Harper
Lee anticipates her novel's
climactic scenes in the
opening sentence of *To
Kill A Mockingbird* (1960).
Foreshadowing draws
overt attention to narrative
as a deliberate construct.

What's yet to come? And what
has already occurred but not yet been revealed?
Foreshadowing and flashbacks are structural
devices writers use to disrupt the beginning-to-
end trajectory of their stories. Hints can be
dropped about future outcomes and scenarios
brought to light from the past that shed light
on the present of the narrative. The technical
term for a flashback is *analepsis*, and
foreshadowing, or a flash-forward, is known as
prolepsis; both are examples of *anachrony*, or
the manipulation of the chronological order of
a text. Flashbacks have long been commonplace
in global literature, across both narrative fiction
and poetry, from Homer's *Odyssey*, in which
Odysseus retrospectively relates his exploits,
to Zadie Smith's *White Teeth* (2000), which
uses flashback to explore the importance of
family history in multi-ethnic communities.
Flashbacks can provide plot-crucial information,
fill in characters' backstories and act as vehicles
for a character's memories. Foreshadowing
appears in two main guises: narrative clues
laying the atmospheric groundwork for some
significant later development, and forthright
statements detailing some specific state of
affairs that has not yet come to pass, as in
Muriel Spark's *The Driver's Seat* (1970): 'She
will be found tomorrow morning dead from
multiple stab-wounds'.

RELATED TOPICS
See also
MODERN LITERATURE
page 24

EPIC POEM
page 82

3-SECOND BIBLIOGRAPHY
'OS LUSÍADAS'
1572
Luís Vaz de Camões

HEART OF DARKNESS
1899
Joseph Conrad

SONS FOR THE RETURN HOME
1973
Albert Wendt

RED SORGHUM
1986
Mo Yan

THE KITE RUNNER
2003
Khaled Hosseini

30-SECOND TEXT
Valerie O'Riordan

*In **To Kill a Mockingbird**,
Scout, the first-person
narrator, warns of some
of the events to come.*

LITERARY STYLES

LITERARY STYLES
GLOSSARY

authorial voice The voice of the author, conveying their unique style and attitude, personality and character. Many authors have such distinctive voices that they can be identified simply by reading a few paragraphs of their work.

Dadaism An artistic movement originating in Switzerland during the First World War, whose primary aim was to ridicule the meaninglessness of the modern world. The writer Hugo Ball founded the movement at the Cabaret Voltaire and he invented the word 'dada' for its childish simplicity.

first-person narrative Any piece of fiction told in the voice of 'I' or 'we', narrated by one person at a time and speaking about himself or herself.

hyperbole A kind of figurative language, not meant to be taken literally, which exaggerates for effect.

hyperreality The idea that life may seem real to us but is no longer real. French theorist Jean Baudrillard postulated that our modern society has replaced all of reality with images and that the human experience is now a simulation of reality. For example, reality television is more real to us than our actual lives. The term also applies to art and literature and how these can now only be produced by reworking existing ideas and cannot ever be original as all original ideas have already been developed.

intertextual This refers to the relationship between two texts, and also the borrowing of text from another source and putting it into the body of your own original work. Authors often use allusion, parody, satire and pastiche as ways of referring to other works. Julia Kristevo, the French semiotician, created the word from the Latin *intertexto*, meaning 'to intermingle while weaving'. She claimed that all texts produced now are intertextual with the texts that came before them, as they will always refer back to what has been written before.

literary minimalism A style of writing characterized by sparseness, simplicity and a lack of extraneous words.

Magic Realism Fiction in which a realistic view of the world is presented alongside some fabulous or impossible events, which are generally accepted without question or remark by the other characters in the book.

metafiction Fiction that flaunts the fact that it is fiction, alluding to literary devices and techniques while telling the story, so as to force the reader to become aware of the artifice of reading.

omniscient narrator The voice in which a story is written, which purports to see inside the heads of all the characters, and to have an overview of all the action – an all-seeing and all-knowing presence. This is the most commonly used storytelling voice.

pastiche A work of literature in a form or style that imitates that of another work in order to celebrate it, unlike parody, which seeks to mock the original.

pidgin English A non-specific name given to any language derived from English, normally in a once-colonized country. When a pidgin vernacular becomes a first language, it is called a Creole.

rhetoric Language intended to have a persuasive or powerful effect, often without meaningful content.

second-person narrative A story in which the voice of the narrator addresses 'you' – either the you of the actual reader or an imagined third person who is addressed as 'you'.

Spanglish A name given to pidgin or Creole languages that blend Spanish and English.

Surrealism An artistic movement started in 1920s New York by the writer André Breton that rejected a rational view of life in favour of one that celebrated the unconscious and dreams, juxtaposing unusual pairings of images and ideas.

technoculture A culture that is informed by its technological activity; also a culture that is very dependent on technology.

third-person narrative A story in which the point of view is written in the third person, for example, he or she. Third-person omniscient narration means the story is told as if the writer can see into all the character's innermost thoughts. Third-person limited narration means that they only represent a single person's thoughts and feelings.

unreliable narrator A device whereby the author uses the narrator of a story to subvert the reader's understanding of the action; the narrator may portray themselves as an honest or reliable source of events but will eventually reveal or be revealed to be otherwise.

NARRATIVE VOICE

the 30-second thesis

A way of describing the speech

and thought patterns of a character or narrator in a work of fiction or poetry, the term 'narrative voice' is literary shorthand for a range of stylistic choices typically associated with characterization. These include not only *how* a character speaks (vocabulary, grammar, dialect) but also *what* they choose to speak about. While first-person narratives like Mark Twain's *Huckleberry Finn* (1885) typically relay only a single voice, third-person narratives, like Virginia Woolf's *Mrs Dalloway* (1925), can allow multiple voices to filter through. Second-person narratives are more unusual: books like Italo Calvino's *If On A Winter's Night A Traveller* (1979) address the reader directly and are frequently associated with literary postmodernism and its critique of realism. Narrative voice is sometimes mixed up with authorial voice, but they're not quite the same: narrative voice applies to one particular character (whether human, non-human or even inanimate) rather then to an author's entire work. Even when a narrator is unnamed and/or omniscient, and apparently unidentifiable, they still have a distinct mode of expression, which we can't assume is consistent with the author's 'real' voice. As with real-life speakers, narrators cannot always be trusted: the unreliable narrator's voice enables him to deceive and manipulate readers.

RELATED TOPICS
See also
POSTCOLONIAL LITERATURE
page 30

REALISM
page 140

POSTMODERNISM
page 148

3-SECOND BIBLIOGRAPHY
THE SOUND AND THE FURY
1929
William Faulkner

THE COLOR PURPLE
1982
Alice Walker

THE WHALE RIDER
1987
Witi Ihimaera

GONE GIRL
2012
Gillian Flynn

30-SECOND TEXT
Valerie O'Riordan

The voice of the narrator – whether omniscient, first-, second- or third-person, sets the tone of a story.

3-SECOND PLOT
Much like a real-life individual's speaking voice, the term narrative voice describes how the narrator expresses him or herself: or, what a text *sounds like*.

3-MINUTE THEME
Narrative voice was a key stylistic device in much twentieth-century postcolonial literature, as writers from dispossessed and marginalized nations and communities eschewed the diction and conventions of literary English (and other languages) in favour of narrative styles that reflected their own heritages: Ken Saro-Wiwa's *Sozaboy* (1985) was written in Nigerian pidgin English, and Puerto-Rican writer Giannina Braschi's *Yo-Yo Boing!* (1998) was the first novel published in Spanglish.

REALISM

the 30-second thesis

Literary realism endeavours to accurately represent everyday life in narrative; it remains popular today, having first appeared in the mid-nineteenth century when British writers like Thomas Hardy and Elizabeth Gaskell instigated a move away from the stylized excesses of Romanticism and Gothic fiction. Realist fiction aims to be unpretentious and objective; its prose style is notable for its focus on specific detail, and its avoidance of rhetorical flourish has frequently allied it with literary minimalism. Proponents of realism shun the implausible and the extraordinary, concentrating instead on the commonplace, often taking as their subject matter the lives of the working classes. Realism is commonly associated with narratives about urban life: a variant from the 1980s, known as dirty realism and associated with Raymond Carver and Pedro Juan Gutiérrez, looks particularly at blue-collar workers and societally marginalized characters. Historically, realist novels have often examined society and politics, with George Eliot's *Middlemarch* (1871–2) looking in forensic detail at confluences of developments in medicine, marriage, education and political reform. Whether it's the apparent simplicity of its prose or its attentiveness to real-world scenarios, realism is always characterized by a deep concern with the believability of the narrative.

3-SECOND PLOT
The attempt to provide, in fiction, an accurate, unembellished and uncensored portrait of humdrum daily life.

3-MINUTE THEME
Some twentieth-century post-structural theorists argued against literary realism, suggesting that it depends upon an assumption we can't prove: that *my* reality definitely matches *your* reality and that we can communicate this reality with words. Critics like Roland Barthes argued that multiple 'realities' co-exist, and what we call 'objective reality' is a cultural construction: literary realism merely presents us with one particular style and tries to pass that off as 'reality'.

RELATED TOPICS
See also
MODERN LITERATURE
page 24

NARRATIVE VOICE
page 138

STREAM OF CONSCIOUSNESS
page 150

3-SECOND BIBLIOGRAPHY
MEMÓRIAS PÓSTUMAS DE BRÁS CUBAS
1881
Joaquim Maria Machado de Assis

THE AGE OF INNOCENCE
1920
Edith Wharton

THE HARP IN THE SOUTH
1948
Ruth Park

A FINE BALANCE
1995
Rohinton Mistry

30-SECOND TEXT
Valerie O'Riordan

Kitchen-sink realism is a literature featuring British working-class characters, often from the north of England.

24 August 1962
Born in Inverness,
Scotland

1980–85
Attended Aberdeen
University

1985–90
PhD at Cambridge
University

1995
*Free Love and Other
Stories* published

2001
Hotel World published
and nominated for the
Booker Prize and the
Orange Prize for Fiction

2005
The Accidental published
and wins Whitbread
Novel of the Year award

2007
Girl Meets Boy published

2011
There But For The
published

2012
Artful published

2014
How to Be Both published

2015
Wins the Costa Novel
Award, Women's Prize for
Fiction and Goldsmiths
Prize for *How to Be Both*

2016
Autumn published (first
of projected Seasonal
Quartet series of novels)

2017
Winter published

2019
Spring published

ALI SMITH

Ali Smith is one of the most inventive and influential writers of today, constantly redefining the boundaries of fiction as we know it. Her ambition is 'to shatter the way we usually see things'. Born in Inverness, one of five children, she grew up on a council estate and went on to study English Literature at the University of Aberdeen. Afterwards she went to Newnham College, Cambridge to write a doctorate in American and Irish modernism; the plays she began writing here were performed at the Edinburgh Fringe and the Cambridge Footlights, which led her to suspend her studies.

In 1995 her first book of short stories, *Free Love and Other Stories*, was published to much acclaim. Her modernist novel *Hotel World* was nominated for the Booker Prize in 2001, bringing her international renown. It is divided into six sections, with five different narrative voices that represent a different aspect of grieving, as well as a different aspect of time. The narrative structure defies convention, employing devices such as stream of consciousness and synecdoche to convey its unique look at life and death. In

How to be Both (2014), which won numerous literary awards, Smith employs a binary narrative: one narrator lives in the present day, the other is a fifteenth-century artist; one could in fact have been invented by the other, as at one point the contemporary narrator writes an essay in the voice of the artist. There are also different printings of the novel, some with the stories in reverse order. This is exactly the kind of playful construct that Smith is famous for.

Themes in this book – and in all of Smith's work – include gender fluidity, same-sex love, interweaving time periods and real contemporary events that invade the fictional narrative. Such an intertextual reality has become particularly important in Smith's seasonal cycle of novels – *Autumn*, *Winter*, *Spring* and the yet-to-be-written Summer – released to coincide with the given season in the year in which they are published, which when complete will form a single multi-volume work. Smith was elected a Fellow of the Royal Society of Literature in 2007, and in 2015 was appointed Commander of the Order of the British Empire for services to literature.

Ella Berthoud

SATIRE
the 30-second thesis

Satire is a form of rhetoric that
is used to expose vices, foibles and foolish or immoral behaviour in individuals, organizations, governments or societies at large, with the aim of enacting or preventing political or social change. Satirists employ various forms of mockery to attack the targets of their displeasure, including wit, hyperbole, irony, sarcasm and outright ridicule. Satire is often humorous, though humour is not an essential component of the art. To be effective, any satire should make the reader feel uncomfortable, encouraging them to reject the behaviour depicted. The use of irony highlights the distance between what is said and what is understood or what is expected and what actually happens. However, the difficulty with this technique is that deliberate ironies can be confused with honest opinion: Mark Twain's *The Adventures of Huckleberry Finn* (1885), for example, has been accused of the racism it aims to reveal. The *Vernon Subutex* trilogy by Virginie Despentes is a satire on modern society, set in Paris. Through the people the protagonist meets, Despentes uses irony to comment on the rise of the far right and the death of intellectualism alongside a range of other issues.

3-SECOND PLOT
Satire uses wit, irony, sarcasm and/or ridicule to expose foolish or immoral behaviour in humans, organizations, governments or society.

3-MINUTE THEME
Parody is often confused with satire. While satire aims to criticize and possibly correct failings in society, parody mimics for comic effect, to entertain and amuse. Parody is the imitation of a writer or genre created by exaggerating traits, as in caricatures. In *Don Quixote* (1615), Cervantes parodies the medieval romance and the chivalric idea of the knight-errant by making the protagonist's quests ridiculous.

RELATED TOPICS
See also
EARLY MODERN LITERATURE
page 22

COMEDY
page 104

IRONY
page 120

3-SECOND BIBLIOGRAPHY
CANDIDE
1759
Voltaire

NORTHANGER ABBEY
1817
Jane Austen

CATCH-22
1961
Joseph Heller

THE SELLOUT
2015
Paul Beatty

30-SECOND TEXT
Naomi Frisby

Mark Twain used satire in many of his novels to highlight uncomfortable issues such as hypocrisy and racism.

GOTHIC

the 30-second thesis

3-SECOND PLOT
The Gothic style conveys
an atmosphere of mystery
and fear, and is mostly
set in castles, with
graveyards, storms and
extreme emotions.

3-MINUTE THEME
In 1976, the scholar Ellen
Moers divided Gothic
literature into the male
and the female genres.
She suggested that those
works written by men are
focused around masculine
transgression of social
taboos, while those written
by women portray the
heroine in flight from an
oppressive male. Male
Gothic aimed to create
horror, while female Gothic
aimed to engender terror;
in female Gothic the
supernatural had a
scientific explanation, in
male the ghosts were real.

Groaning with castles, ruins,
vampires and moonlit graveyards, Gothic
literature began with Horace Walpole's playfully
frightening *The Castle of Otranto* (1764).
Including elements of the supernatural, high
emotion, labyrinths, madness and miraculous
survivals, all set around Gothic architecture, it
was the catalyst for a writing style that thrives
to this day. Gothic overlaps significantly with
horror; Gothic literature establishes a mood
of fear, creating an eerie atmosphere that is
unsettling rather than gruesome. Gothic tales
commonly employ foreshadowing in the form
of visions, omens and curses. Superstitious
portents such as black cats, broken mirrors and
nightmares might predict an unfortunate series
of events. The English Romantic poets were
drawn to the heightened emotional states of
the style, with John Keats' utilizing it in his long,
narrative poem *The Eve of St Agnes* (1820). Lord
Byron hosted a ghost-story writing competition
in 1816 that sparked the creation of one of
literature's Gothic masterpieces, Mary Shelley's
Frankenstein (1818). The Brontë sisters in the
mid-nineteenth century also brought Gothic
elements into their writing, as the intense
circumstances afforded by the genre allowed
their female characters to behave in non-
conformist ways at odds with patriarchal society.

RELATED TOPICS
See also
HORROR
page 48

MELODRAMA
page 108

FORESHADOW & FLASHBACK
page 132

3-SECOND BIBLIOGRAPHY
THE DEVIL'S ELIXIRS
1815
E.T.A. Hoffman

DRACULA
1897
Bram Stoker

WIDE SARGASSO SEA
1966
Jean Rhys

BELOVED
1987
Toni Morrison

30-SECOND TEXT
Ella Berthoud

*The Gothic aesthetic in
literature is characterized
by an air of foreboding
and a sense of the
macabre.*

POSTMODERNISM

the 30-second thesis

3-SECOND PLOT
Postmodernism is a broad range of literary styles that question the idea of objective truth, reality, morality and reason, considering them to be socially constructed.

3-MINUTE THEME
Postmodernism was a movement across the disciplines of art, literature, film, music, drama, architecture, history and philosophy during the mid-to-late twentieth century. Artists and writers associated with Dadaism and Surrealism, such as Hannah Höch and André Breton, influenced the development of Postmodern literature. Their playful use of collage, chance and parody, their desire to challenge the authority of the artist through exploring the subconscious mind, influenced literary writers in their approach to texts.

Postmodernism encompasses a broad range of literary styles and ideas, linked by their reaction to the preceding Modernist movement. The common tropes of postmodern literature, which were prominent from the mid- to the late-twentieth century, include the age-old use of text acknowledging the reader, recognizing the role they play in responding to the work; while metafiction is often used to draw attention to the work as a piece of storytelling. For example, *The Golden Notebook* (1962) by Doris Lessing, employs five notebooks in which the protagonist Anna Wulf records her life. Interspersed with these are seemingly realistic sections from Anna's life that overlap and interact with the diary entries. Although any list of features commonly found in the postmodern novel can never be exhaustive, as the movement inherently resists definition, they include: texts being often fragmented or non-linear; the use of 'intertextual' conversations; pastiche combining different styles or genres within one text; irony and black humour; technoculture and hyperreality examining the role of capitalism; and Magic Realism employing magical or supernatural elements to explore the political and human state, as in Isabel Allende's novel of postcolonial Latin America, *The House of the Spirits* (1982).

RELATED TOPICS
See also
THEATRE OF THE ABSURD
page 110

NARRATIVE VOICE
page 138

3-SECOND BIBLIOGRAPHY
LIFE: A USER'S MANUAL
1978
Georges Perec

IF ON A WINTER'S NIGHT A TRAVELLER
1979
Italo Calvino

BLOOD AND GUTS IN HIGH SCHOOL
1984
Kathy Acker

THE WIND-UP BIRD CHRONICLE
1997
Haruki Murakami

30-SECOND TEXT
Naomi Frisby

Postmodern literature makes the reader self-consciously aware of the act of reading.

STREAM OF CONSCIOUSNESS

the 30-second thesis

A narrative technique that aims

to mimic the uninhibited flow of its characters' thoughts as they occur, stream of consciousness differs from other narrative modes in its move away from conventionally 'correct' grammar, punctuation and syntax. Its non-linear, fragmented and associative style aims to approximate the actual experience of thinking; in fact, the very term 'stream of consciousness' was coined by an American psychologist (William James) rather than a literary theorist. As a prose style, however, it's often seen as experimental and difficult, largely through association with the literary modernists who pioneered it. Writers like James Joyce, with *Ulysses* (1922), used stream of consciousness in order to place their readers as close as possible to the workings of their characters' minds, complete with messy impressions and distractions: 'Open your eyes now. I will. One moment. Has all vanished since? If I open and am for ever in the black adiaphane. *Basta!*' As European and American modernism lost popular ground to postmodernism (which was less concerned with interiority), stream of consciousness fell out of fashion. It has, however, re-emerged in the twenty-first century, with writers such as Eimear McBride using this fragmentation to explore the collapse of language under the pressure of violence and trauma.

3-SECOND PLOT
Stream of consciousness is a literary technique that seeks to reproduce on the page the chaos, the unpredictability and the associative diversions of actual thoughts.

3-MINUTE THEME
Stream of consciousness lends itself to dissidence due to its rejection of convention and order. While it's often associated with European literary modernism (Dorothy Richardson, Virginia Woolf), it has a rich pedigree around the world, from the short fiction of Assamese writer Saurav Kumar Chaliha (jailed in 1950 for his involvement with the Revolutionary Communist Party of India) and Zimbabwean novelist Charles Mungoshi's *Ndiko Kupindana Kwamazuva* (1975), whose anti-colonial works were banned by the Rhodesian government.

RELATED TOPICS
See also
MODERNIST LITERATURE
page 28

FORESHADOW & FLASHBACK
page 132

NARRATIVE VOICE
page 138

3-SECOND BIBLIOGRAPHY
NOTES FROM UNDERGROUND
1864
Fyodor Dostoyevsky

TENDER BUTTONS
1914
Gertrude Stein

AMULET
1999
Roberto Bolaño

HOW STELLA GOT HER GROOVE BACK
1996
Terry McMillan

30-SECOND TEXT
Valerie O'Riordan

Virginia Woolf's **Mrs Dalloway** *depicts the consciousnesses of a large cast of characters in London on a single day.*

APPENDICES

RESOURCES

BOOKS

Poetics
Aristotle
(Penguin Classics, 1996)

The Seven Basic Plots:
Why We Tell Stories
Christopher Booker
(Continuum, 2005)

The Book of Forgotten Authors
Christopher Fowler
(Quercus, 2017)

Mythologies
Roland Barthes
(Hill & Wang, 1973)

The Art of Fiction
David Lodge
(Vintage, 2011)

A Glossary of Literary Terms
M. H. Abrams and Geoffrey Harpham
(Wadsworth Publishing; 10th edn, 2011)

The Elements of Eloquence:
How to Turn the Perfect English Phrase
Mark Forsyth
(Icon Books, 2016)

An Introduction to Literature
Criticism and Theory
Andrew Bennet
(Routledge, 5th edn, 2016)

The Poetry Handbook
John Lennard
(Oxford Unversity Press, 2nd edn, 2006)

The Ode Less Travelled:
Unlocking the Poet Within
Stephen Fry
(Arrow, 2007)

A Little History of Literature
John Sutherland
(Yale University Press, 2013)

History of the Theatre
Oscar G. Brockett and Franklin J. Hildy
(Pearson, 10th edn, 2007)

Global Literary Theory: an Anthology
ed. Richard J. Lane
(Routledge 2013)

The Norton Anthology of
Theory and Criticism
(W. W. Norton, 2nd edn, 2010)

Literature: Why it Matters
Robert Eaglestone
(Polity Press, 2019)

What is World Literature?
David Damrosch
(Princeton University Press, 2003)

An Ecology of World Literature
Alexander Beecroft
(Verso Books, 2015)

WEBSITES

The Times Literary Supplement
https://www.the-tls.co.uk/latest-edition/

The Paris Review Daily
https://www.theparisreview.org/blog/

The New Yorker
https://www.newyorker.com/magazine

The Millions
https://themillions.com/about-the-millions

NOTES ON CONTRIBUTORS

CONSULTANT

Ella Berthoud studied English Literature at Cambridge University and went on to the University of East London to study Fine Art. She has worked as an artist in residence at HM Pentonville Prison, at Friends' School Saffron Walden and at Queenswood School in Hertfordshire. In 2007, Ella and Susan Elderkin developed the idea of bibliotherapy – prescribing literature for ailments – in conjunction with The School of Life. Ella and Susan co-authored *The Novel Cure: An A-Z of Literary Remedies* and *The Story Cure: How to Keep Kids Happy, Healthy and Wise*. Ella has since written *The Art of Mindful Reading: Embracing the Wisdom of Words*.

Lucien Young studied English at Selwyn College, Cambridge, where he was a member of the world-famous Footlights comedy group, as well as a contributor to *Varsity*. A television writer with credits including BBC Three's *Siblings* and *Murder in Successville*, Lucien is also a poet and the author of four books, including three works of political literary satire and *#Sonnets*, published in October 2019, which looks at some of the trashiest aspects of contemporary life via the exacting disciplines of the Shakespearean sonnet.

Valerie O'Riordan is a fiction writer and lecturer in Creative Writing at the University of Bolton. She has also taught at the University of Manchester, where she completed her PhD on the narrativization of trauma in the post-9/11 short story cycle. She has published on narrative form in the works of Ali Smith and A.L. Kennedy, and her short fiction has appeared in *Tin House*, *The Manchester Review* and *LitMag*. She was a winner of the O. Henry Award in 2019 and is working on a novel funded by Arts Council England. She is Senior Editor of *The Forge Literary Magazine* and Executive Editor of *The Bolton Review*. She is particularly interested in working-class representation and hybrid forms in contemporary British and Irish fiction.

Naomi Frisby is a doctoral candidate in Creative Writing at Sheffield Hallam University. She has written on a variety of topics for *OZY*, *Fiction Uncovered* and the Waterstones' blog, as well as appearing on Radio 3's *Free Thinking*. She regularly chairs literary events for festivals and for Waterstones. Her short fiction has been shortlisted for *The White Review* Short Story Prize and longlisted for the Manchester Fiction Prize.

Charlotte Raby is a writer and educational consultant who is currently advising the Department for Education. She works with publishers, schools, universities and parents to develop resources and policy about early reading and the teaching of English. She is an advocate of reading for pleasure and regularly speaks at conferences about the importance of reading. She has written hundreds of educational resources, teaching programmes and children's books for schools and home learning. She writes regular articles and blogs about reading, vocabulary and children's literature.

Lauren de Sá Naylor is a writer, artist and educator based in West Yorkshire. She did her Masters in Critical and Cultural Theory at the University of Leeds and teaches contextual studies at Salford University.

INDEX

A

Adichie, Chimamanda Ngozi 72–3, 126
Agbabi, Patience 86
alienation 12
allegory 12, 122
anachrony 118, 130
analepsis 118, 130
anon 80
anthropomorphism 119, 128
apostrophe 80, 88
Apuleius: The Golden Ass 52
Aristophanes 104, 106–7
Aristotle 102, 104, 119
Aryan 12, 18
Asante tales 128
Ashvaghosa 18
Atwood, Margaret 42, 50
authorial voice 136, 138
auto-fiction 64, 70
autobiographies 70
autonomous characters 64
avant-garde 100

B

ballads 92
Beowulf 20, 82
Bible, the 76, 84, 122
bibliomancy 80, 91
Bildungsroman 34, 58
Blake, William 24
Blume, Judy 58
bodice rippers 35, 54
Book of the Dead 16
Books of Hours 20
Borges, Jorge Luis 119, 124–5
Brecht, Bertolt 114
Buddha, Gautama 74
Bulgakov, Mikhail: *The Master and Margarita* 122

C

cadence 80
catharsis 100, 102
chapbooks 36

Chaucer, Geoffrey: *Canterbury Tales* 20, 36, 126
children's literature 24, 40, 128
clowning 101
Coehlo, Paul: *The Alchemist* 122
comedy 104
Confucius 74
crime fiction 44
cuneiform script 13, 16

D

Dadaism 136, 148
dialogic texts 35, 38
diaries 68
Dickens, Charles 24, 56, 70
dirty realism 140
dissidents 64
Doolittle, Hilda 26–7
Dostoevsky, Fyodor 24, 46–7
Doyle, Arthur Conan 44
drabbles 65
dramatic irony 119
dribbles 65
dystopian fiction 50

E

early modern literature 22
Eliot, T.S.: *The Waste Land* 28, 128
Elizabethan era 81
Enheduanna 16
epic narratives/verses 12, 36, 82
Epic of Gilgamesh 16, 42, 82
epic theatre 101
epistolary novels 38
eutopias 50
exegesis 65
existentialism 64, 74

F

fables 64, 66, 118
fairy tales 22, 24

fantasy fiction 52
farces 100
Fielding, Henry: *Shamela* 38
first-person narratives 137
flash fiction 64, 65, 66
flashbacks 130
flintlock 34, 52
folklore 34
foreshadowing 130
forum theatre 114
fragmented narratives 12, 28
framed tales 64
free verse 84

G

ghazal, the 96
gijinka/gijinhō 118, 128
Goethe, Johann Wolfgang von 24, 76
Gothic style 146
graphic novels 56
grimdark 34, 52
guerrilla theatre 100, 114
Gutenberg Parenthesis 12, 14

H

Hafez-de-Chiraz 90–1, 96
haiga 94
haiku 94
heroic couplets 81, 86
Hinton, S.E.: *The Outsiders* 58
historical novels 40
Homer 30, 82, 122, 130
Horace 88, 120
Horatian satire 104
Horation odes 80, 88
horror 48
humanism 118
hyperbole 136
hyperreality 136, 148

I

iambic pentameters 80, 86
Illiad, The 30, 82, 122
Instapoets 80, 84

intertextual relationships 137, 148
invisible theatre 101, 114
irony 120, 144

J

Joyce, James 28, 150
Juvenalian satire 104

K

Kālidāsa 18
kāvya 12, 18
King, Stephen: *The Shining* 48
Kipling, Rudyard 30
kuhi 80, 94

L

Lampedusa, Giuseppe Tomasi di: *The Leopard* 40
Laozi: *Tao Te Ching* 16
Lee, Harper: *To Kill a Mockingbird* 130
Lewis, Wyndham 28
LGBTQ+ literature 60
libri gialli 44
literary minimalism 137
Living Theatre, The 114
lyric poems 81

M

Magic Realism 52, 137, 148
mahākāvya 18
manga 56
Mantel, Hilary: *Wolf Hall* 40, 120
Marlowe, Christopher 22, 102
medieval literature 20
melodrama 108
memoirs 13, 70
metafiction 137
metre 81
microfiction 64, 66
Milton, John: *Paradise Lost* 22, 76,
mime 101
minisagas 65
mnemonic devices 13

modernism 28, 150
monologic texts 35, 38
Moore, Marianne 84
morality plays 100
More, Sir Thomas: *Utopia* 50
mytho-fantasy 34, 42
mythology 34

N
Nanak, Guru 74
narrative voice 138
nasībs 96
Newton, Isaac 74
Nietzsche, Friedrich 64, 74
non-fiction novels 65
novellas 34, 36
novels 22, 36 *see also* individual
  types

O
O'Connor, Frank 66
Oberammergau 112
odes 88
Odyssey, The 82
omniscient narrators 137
oral tradition 14, 18
orality 13
Orwell, George: *Animal Farm* 128
Ovid: *Metamorphoses* 52
Owen, Wilfred 28, 120

P
Panchatantra 118, 128
Parables 119, 122
paradigms 100
parody 101, 144
Passion plays 112
pastiche 137, 148
patois 13, 30
Perrault, Charles 22
personification 128
Petrarch 86
Petronius: *The Satyricon* 60
philosophical works 65, 74
pidgin English 137, 138

Pindar 88
placards 101
Plato 16, 74
Poe, Edgar Allan 44
political theatre 114
polylogic texts 35, 38
postcolonial literature 30, 138
postmodernism 148
Pound, Ezra 27, 28, 84
pratfalls 100
progenitors 35
prolepsis 118, 130
psalms 13
pulp fiction 35

Q
qasidas 96
Qur'an, the 76

R
Rambhadracharya, Jagadguru 82
Ramlila of Ramnagar 112
Realism 24, 28, 140
register 80
religious texts 76
renga 81
Restoration, the 80
rhetoric 119
rhetorical devices 81
rhyme schemes 81
Rokeya, Begum 42
romance 35, 54
Romanticism 13, 24, 81

S
Saikaku 22
San Pedro, Diego de: *Prison of
  Love* 38
Sanskrit 13, 18, 104
sarcasm 119, 120
Sartre, Jean Paul 64, 74
satire 104, 144
science fiction 42
Scott, Sir Walter 40, 92
second-person narratives 137

Sewell, Anna: *Black Beauty* 128
Shakespeare, William 22, 86,
  102, 104, 126
Shastri, Satya Vrat 18
Shaw, George Bernard:
  Pygmalion 120
Shintoism 119, 128
short stories 66
short-short fiction 65, 66
Singh, Jagjit 96
*Sir Gawain and the Green
  Knight* 20
Smith, Ali 142–3
Smith, Zadie: *White Teeth* 130
sonnets 86
Soyinka, Wole 102
Spanglish 137, 138
Spanish Inquisition 35, 48
speculative fiction 35, 42
Spiegelman, Art: *Maus* 56
St. Aubyn, Edward 65
stanzas 81
steampunk 35, 52
Stein, Gertrude 70
stream of consciousness 28, 150
Sturm und Drang 13, 24
sudden fiction 65
Sumerians 16, 42, 48
Surrealism 137, 148
Suzuki, Koji: *Ring* 48
Swift, Jonathan: *Gulliver's
  Travels* 22
symbolism 126

T
Ta'ziyeh 112
Tan, Shaun: *The Arrival* 56
technocultures 137, 148
Theatre of the Absurd 110
Theatre of the Oppressed 114
third-person narratives 137
Thoreau, Henry David 70
Tolkien, J.R.R. 52
Tolstoy, Leo 24
tragedy 102

travel journals 65, 68
Tudor Court 81, 86
twitterature 65

U
Übermensch 64, 74
Ultraists 119, 125
unreliable narrators 38, 137, 138
utopian fiction 50

V
vaudeville 100
Vedic literature 12, 14, 18
verbal irony 119
vers libre 84
Virgil: *Aeneid* 82, 126
voltas 80

W
Webtoons 35, 56
Whitman, Walt: *Leaves of
  Grass* 84
Williams, William Carlos 27, 84
Wu Tsao 60

Y
Yoruba 101
young adult fiction 58, 60

Z
zeitgeist 54
Zola, Émile 24

ACKNOWLEDGEMENTS

The publisher would like to thank the following for permission to reproduce copyright material on the following pages:

Alamy/ AF archive: 133; age fotostock: 95; Archive World: 52; Atomic: 109; bilwissedition Ltd. & Co. KG: 55; Chronicle: 2, 127; Classic Image: 90; Cultural Archive: 109; dpa picture alliance: 69, 73; Everett Collection Inc: 26, 121; FOR ALAN: 105; Geraint Lewis: 142; GL Archive: 69; Granger Historical Picture Archive: 25; Keith Corrigan: 49, 97; Niday Picture Library: 6, 37; Pictorial Press Ltd: 124; Rich Dyson: 111; Tim Whitby: 69; United Archives GmbH: 44; Universal Art Archive: 9, 151

Bundesarchiv, Bild 183-24300-0049 / Sturm, Horst: 115

Dreamstime/ Branko Grujic: 89; Bratty1206: 17; Oleg Kravchuk: 149

Folger Shakespeare Library: 87

Getty/ duncan1890: 77; Hulton Archive: 121; Richard Westall: 83

The Graphics Fairy: 2, 75, 127

Internet Archive/ Missouri Botanical Garden: 25

Lawrence J Schoneberg Collection of Manuscripts, Kislak Center for Special Collections, Rare Books and Manuscripts, University of Pennsylvania: 97

Library of Congress: 6, 15, 21, 37, 67, 89, 113, 139

Shutterstock/ 3d imagination: 29; 9'63 Creation: 7, 57; aaabbbccc: 121; Agustina Camilion; akimov konstantin: 17; Alex Leo: 57; ALYOHAE: 95; ananaline: 67; Anastasia Lembrik: 55; andrea crisante: 50; Andrea Izzotti: 17; Anne Mathiasz: 77; Authentic travel: 31; Avprophoto: 95; ayzek: 69; Beketoff: 29; Ben_Stevens: 57; bjphotographs: 123; BlackMac: 17; Bob Orsillo: 43; Buntoon Rodseng: 15; canan kaya: 19; chai na phon phochadee: 67; charles taylor: 43; cherezoff: 75; chippix: 23; Christian Mueller: 57; Cris Foto: 15; cziegelberg: 52; davide versaci: 147; Digital abstract Art: 43; Digital Storm: 52; durantelallera: 57; DutchScenery: 133; ELAKSHI CREATIVE BUSINESS: 19; Everett - Art: 52, 87, 129; Everett Collection: 39, 43, 44, 49, 50, 75, 85, 93, 107, 109, 111, 115, 129, 131, 133, 139, 145, 147, 149; Everett Historical: 9, 29, 31, 37, 41, 61, 69, 85, 89, 95, 121, 141, 145, 151; Ezume Images: 9, 151; file404: 59; Filip Fuxa: 2, 127; frankie's: 67; Frazer: 37; Georgios Kollidas: 23, 105, 113; Georgios Tsichlis: 105; Gideon7: 131; good_mood: 50; Haali: 77; HAKKI ARSLAN: 50; Hein Nouwens: 9, 41, 69, 147, 149, 151;

Hoika Mikhail: 83; hurricanehank: 15; iABC: 139; Ioan Panaite: 129; itechno: 83; iulias: 147; Ivan Ponomarev: 61; James R T Bossert: 44; Jason Vandehey: 145; KEEP GOING: 55; kenkuza: 115; KennyK.com: 57; ketrinkin1: 55; Kristo Robert: 50; Krivosheev Vitaly: 83; Kuznetsov Alexey: 39; legacy1995: 83; LightField Studios: 61; Lightspring: 93; Lorna Roberts: 121; Lucian Coman: 129; Manekina Serafima: 129; Marek Poplawski: 9, 151; marekuliasz: 87; Marish: 93; Martin M303: 59; Marzolino: 9, 49, 151; matrioshka: 57; Mazur Travel: 31; Menno Schaefer: 89; mhatzapa: 77; Mike McDonald: 77; Mikhail Leonov: 133; Morphart Creation: 75, 77, 83, 105, 111; Nadiinko: 131; Nagel Photography: 145; naKornCreate: 50; Neil Lang: 9, 151; Neirfy: 111; Neveshkin Nikolay: 25; Nice Shutterstock: 75; Nor Gal: 95; NORTHERN IMAGERY: 97; Olga Nikonova: 44; Oliver Hoffmann: 139; one line man: 85; Patricia Hofmeester: 109; pavila: 89; Pawel Horazy: 129; PawelG Photo: 131; Perfect Vecors: 149: Peter Hermes Furian: 115; Peteri: 41; pio3: 2, 127; Pixeljoy: 77, 123; posztos: 145; Priymak Evgeniy: 123; Rakic: 61; Redshinestudio: 61; RetroClipArt: 43; Rolling Orange: 17; Sabphoto: 59, 131; Scorpp: 87; seezcape: 41; Sergej Razvodovskij: 133; Sergey Goryachev: 123; Shelli Jensen: 31; Sigur: 131; SilverCircle: 89; SongPixels: 23; SpeedKingz: 59; StockImageFactory.com: 19; Studiojumpee: 15; Susan Schmitz: 129; SvetlanaSF: 75; Tatiana Popova: 2, 127; the palms: 93; thenatchdl: 61; Tymonko Galyna: 39, 89; VanReeel: 77; Venzy: 107; Victor Z: 2, 127; Victorian Traditions: 55; Vikoshkina: 93; VladisChern: 31; vladm: 9, 151; wenani: 111; Yurii Zymovin: 49; Zacarias Pereira da Mata: 147; Zack Frank: 71

Vintage Printable: 111

Wellcome Collection: 19, 21, 93, 113, 129

Wikimedia Commons: 21, 39, 46, 57, 59, 69, 71, 77, 93, 108, 123, 129, 131, 139, 141; art renewal center: 25; BabelStone: 83; BritishLibrary: 21; By Gorupdebesanez: 115; FOTO:FORTEPAN / Hegedus Judit: 23; New York Public Library: 23

All reasonable efforts have been made to trace copyright holders and to obtain their permission for the use of copyright material. The publisher apologizes for any errors or omissions in the list above and will gratefully incorporate any corrections in future reprints if notified.